Lillian Beckwith was born in Ellesmere Port, Cheshire, in 1916. Her father's grocery shop provided the background for her autobiographical book *About My Father's Business,* which describes a 1920s family from a child's viewpoint.

She went to live in the Hebrides before the Second World War and stayed for nearly twenty years. Her hilarious initiation into crofting life is captured in the heart-warming book *The Hills Is Lonely.* She acquired her own cottage, and living and working on her own croft gave rise to her series of magical Hebridean books such as *The Sea for Breakfast.* She now lives on the Isle of Man.

Lightly Poached

Lillian Beckwith

HOUSE OF
STRATUS

This edition published in 2002 by House of Stratus, an imprint of
House of Stratus Ltd, Thirsk Industrial Park, York Road, Thirsk,
North Yorkshire, YO7 3BX, UK.
Also at: House of Stratus Inc., 2 Neptune Road, Poughkeepsie, NY 12601, USA.

www.houseofstratus.com

Typeset, printed and bound by House of Stratus.

A catalogue record for this book is available from the British Library
and The Library of Congress.

ISBN 0-7551-0275-4

For Philip, Katy, Tina, Neil and Anita

Contents

Vocabulary

Cailleach	*Old woman*	Kyle-yak
Mo ghaoil	*My dear*	Mo gale
Ceilidh	*An impromptu meeting for gossip and song*	Cayley
Strupach	*A cup of tea and a bite to eat*	Stroopak
Oidhche mhath!	*Good night*	Oi she-va
Bodach	*Old man*	Bodak
Biolaire	*Watercress*	Byul-ar
Thig a 's Tigh	*Come inside*	Hic-a-Stoya
Thalla	*Go away!*	Halla
Seanachaidh	*A teller of tales*	Shenna-ka
Sao	*Here, take it*	Sho
Potach	*Oatmeal mixed with water and pressed into a round cake*	Pot-ak
Gogaid	*A light-headed, foolish girl*	Go-gad

Orra Chomais	*'An amulet to deprive a man of his v.r.l.ty particularly on his wedding night, by way of vengeance (A fine thing to cure blackguards!)'* Ad literam *MacAlpine's Gaelic dictionary*	Orra-shoma
Each Uisge	*Waterhorse*	Ek-ooska
Tha e breagh	*It is fine (Good day!)*	He Breeah
Crack	*A gossipy chat*	
Sooyan	*A young coalfish*	

Lightly Poached

The sun-stained showers had put a sheen on everything. On the summer grass; on the craggy hills; on the gulls' wings; on the sibilant water and on the rocks of the shore. Even the clouds looked as if they had been polished up with a soft duster.

Between the showers I had been engaged on the urgent task of cleaning my weed-smothered potato patch, using a hoe until my aching shoulders entreated rest when I would crouch down and pull out the weeds by hand until my knees reminded me it was time to stand up and use the hoe again. I loathed weeding potatoes. As each spring came round and I, helped by neighbouring crofters, set the seed on nests of manure along the new-dug furrows I vowed that this year I would really cherish my potatoes; that I would attend to the weeding as soon as the green rosettes appeared above the soil and would continue regularly doing a little every fine day so that, come summer, I should have a trim forest of healthy green shaws rising from the ridged black earth with a definable space, weed free and wide enough for a booted foot to tread, between each row. Thus, I promised myself, I would ensure that when the time came for harvesting I should, like my neighbours, fill pail after pail, sack after sack, with potatoes of a size that could reasonably be termed 'ware', that is, fist-sized or larger. So far, however, even the most encouraging critics would never have described my potato crop as anything but 'seed', which means of a size equivalent to a bantam's egg, or worse, as 'chats', which were hardly bigger than marbles or, as Morag, my ex-landlady, described them, as 'bein' no bigger than a hen would swallow in one gulp'. Too small for cooking in their jackets, they had to be peeled raw and anyone who has had to endure winter after winter of coping with such puny runts will know there is no more dispiriting an occupation. I usually ended up by boiling a panful every day, mashing them with a bottle and mixing them with oatmeal and then feeding them to my cow and hens while, swallowing my pride, I would buy a sack of potatoes from someone who had worked much more dedicatedly than I and who therefore had some to spare. Alas this year again despite all my resolutions and the tactful comments of well-meaning Bruachites I had failed to get to grips with the task of weeding in time and now in midsummer except for two short rows which I had cleaned the previous morning my potato patch resembled a jungle more than an orderly forest and with the plants scarcely a hand's height the leaves had already begun to pale as a result of their contest with lusty persicary, binding buttercups and tenacious dockens. I knew they must be rescued now or never, so, ignoring my body's unwillingness and the clouds of midges which assailed me every time the breeze died and a shower threatened to obscure the sun, I continued resolutely, hoping that I could clean enough rows to yield sufficient ware potatoes for my own use. Another hour's work, I told myself, and then I could finish for the day. As I made the resolution I sighed forgetfully which resulted in my having to spit out a queue of midges which had been hovering around my mouth waiting the opportunity to explore my larynx. Kneeling down I resumed pulling at the strangle of corn spurrey which, though relatively easy to uproot, leaves a sticky deposit on the hands which proves even more attractive to predatory insects than clean flesh. I wished often that potatoes were not so essential a part of my food supplies, but to face a Bruach winter without a good store of potatoes in the barn would have been foolhardy. The crofters would have considered it suicidal.

It had been some time now since the last shower; some time since I had had an excuse to nip back for a 'fly cuppie' in the coolth and comfort of the cottage. Through my thin blouse the sun was toasting my back; the exposed parts of my body itched with midge bites; my open-toed sandals – open-toed due not to design but to wear – were full of earth and sharp grit. I was sticky, dirty, itchy and achy and I longed for a respite. Straightening up I rested on the hoe. The breeze had died away completely with the last shower, leaving shreds of mist in the corries of the hills. The sea was like a stretch of blue cambric variegated with darker patches which, suddenly erupting into arrow-shaped shockwaves of spray, told of shoals of mackerel pursuing their food around the bay.

'So you're busy!' It was Morag's voice and I turned to greet her as she tacked across the croft towards me. Accompanying Morag was Flora, a remote kinswoman of hers who occasionally visited Bruach on holiday from the East Coast fishing port where she lived. Flora was famous in Bruach as being one of a band of 'kipper lassies', the girls who travelled from port to port throughout the herring season and in all weathers sat out on the piers deftly gutting and cleaning mountains of herring newly unloaded from the fishing boats; bandying ribald pleasantries with the crews and, reputedly, screaming imprecations with complete impartiality at sluggard fish porters, scouting gulls or indeed anyone who threatened to impede their work. Flora took great pride in being a 'kipper lassie' and always carried around with her a photograph cut from a newspaper which showed her along with half a dozen other lassies smilingly busy at their gutting and seemingly oblivious of the hail and sleet that flew around them. There was an inked ring round Flora on the photograph because the girls were so bundled up in clothes that identification might otherwise have been impossible. She was middle-aged, 'all beam and bust' as Erchy described her, and her eyes and hair were appropriately kipper-coloured. Her voice was as strident as a ship's siren; her laughter piercing and when irritated her vocabulary would, according to an admiring Hector, 'take the feathers off a hoody-crow'. She was a good-natured, good-humoured soul and whilst she was in Bruach the summer ceilidhs were enlivened by lurid accounts of her adventures, quarrels, flirtations and spending sprees, accounts which I no doubt would have found more entertaining had I been able to decode more than one word in six of her broad East Coast speech and that one word usually 'yon'. In her absence the Bruachites referred to her as to all 'kipper lassies' as 'Skin-a-herrin' Lizzie', though they would never have been either discourteous or rash enough to have used the nickname in her hearing. Only once did I hear it used in her presence and that was by Davy, a Glasgow-bred child without a vestige of Gaelic courtesy or reticence who with his mother was visiting a relative in the village. One Friday evening when there had been the usual batch of customers, adults and children, waiting at the weekly grocery van for their turn to be served Davy was there insolently superintending his doting mother's purchases to ensure she bought for him an ample supply of sweeties and biscuits. When Flora appeared he had left his mother abruptly, sidled round to the front of the van and begun chanting:

'Skin-a-herrin',
Skin-a-herrin',
Skin-a-herrin',
Lizzie.'

In the unthinkable event of a Bruach child behaving in such a fashion the nearest adult male would have grabbed him, boxed his ears and been thanked by the embarrassed parents for administering punishment so promptly. But Davy was a foreigner and though we were all made to feel exceedingly uncomfortable by the boy's rudeness only old Murdoch admonished him with a snapped 'Whist, boy!' and the gesture of an upraised hand. Davy ignored the old man and continued his taunting. Flora darted a glance at the mother as if giving her a chance to take action before she herself did, but the mother had retreated into an air of intense preoccupation with the small print on a packet of cream crackers and would not look up. We saw Flora's bosom swell; we saw her eyes glint and we prepared to flinch at the linguistic dexterity we expected to hear. But our ears were assailed by no fish-pier malediction. Instead Flora merely raised her voice to its most penetrating pitch and screamed: 'Aye, lad, I can skin a herrin' as quick and clean as your own mother skins the lodgers that stay in your house!'

The delighted smiles on the faces of the Bruachites were swiftly erased as Davy's mother turned first on Flora and then on the rest of us a look of concentrated venom that changed even as we watched to confusion as she realised that, isolated as Bruach was, it was not too isolated for us to be unaware of the poor reputation of the boarding house she kept in the city and that lodgers who had once endured her hard beds, scanty food and high prices never stayed long. Calling her son with an asperity that startled him into obedience she hurried him away.

'He's a wee monster, that one,' Anna Vic had said severely.

'An' his father before him,' observed someone else.

Old Murdoch took his pipe out of his mouth. 'As the old cock crows, so the young one learns,' he had declared fatalistically.

'I'm thinkin' it's wastin' your time you are, mo ghaoil, cleanin' your potatoes when there's showers about. You're no' givin' the weeds a chance to die.' Morag was standing by my potato patch assessing its chances of survival with much the same expression on her face as if she were standing by a deathbed. 'You should get at them when the ground's good and dry.'

The thought that much of my day's labour might have been in vain was a little deflating but I rallied when I remembered I had carried away most of the uprooted weeds to the dung heap behind the byre where they could revive or perish without harming my potatoes. Nevertheless it was with relief that I abandoned the hoe.

'Me an' Flora,' continued Morag, 'was thinkin' we'd go down to the shore an' see maybe will we get a wee bitty dulse. The tide's right for it now.'

We looked down at the sea-deserted, weed-covered rocks, assimilating the prospects of dulse picking.

'Oh, yes. It's pretty low tides this week,' I agreed, confident now of my knowledge of the sea and its movements.

Flora gave me a kipper-coloured glance. 'D'ye like yon?' she asked with a vigorous nod towards the sea.

'Dulse, do you mean?' I was constantly being nonplussed by Flora's haphazard 'yons'.

'Aye, yon.'

'No,' I confessed. 'I've never managed to acquire a taste for it.' To me dulse tasted like strips of rubber steeped in water that had been used for washing fishy plates.

'Octh, yon's good, yon,' she commented ecstatically.

'Erchy brought us a skart just the other day and Flora has a fancy for a wee bitty dulse boiled along with it,' explained Morag.

'He gave me a skart, too,' I told her. 'He must have been feeling generous.'

'Generous?' echoed Morag. 'Did you not notice he's lost his teeths an' canna eat them himself?'

'Oh, of course,' I admitted, remembering Erchy's gummy embarrassment when he had come to bestow his gift and his subsequent hasty departure in spite of the tea I offered.

'It will be six months he'll need to wait till the dentist comes again unless he goes up to Inverness himself to get a new set,' Morag announced. 'An' six months is a long time to be without your teeths once you're used to havin' them,' she added.

'He told me he'd lost them overboard when they were fishing,' I said.

'Indeed it was the truth he was tellin' you,' agreed Morag with the flicker of a smile.

'Well, I wouldn't wish Erchy discomfort but they say it's an ill wind,' I said lightly. 'And it seems a long time since I last tasted skart.'

'An' had he yours skinned for you?' asked Morag.

'Oh, yes,' I replied. 'I doubt if I could have done that for myself.' A skart or shag is prepared for cooking not by plucking but by skinning it like a rabbit and then the thick red meat can be cut from its breast like steak. There was normally so much meat on one that, casseroled, a bird would provide me with four good meals and there would still be stock for soup. 'It was last Tuesday he gave me mine and I'm just about at the end of it now,' I told her.

'Aye, I believe it was Tuesday we got ours,' agreed Morag. 'I mind him sayin' he got three that day.'

'And you haven't cooked it yet?' I asked. It was now the following Monday and as Bruach boasted no such conveniences as refrigerators I doubted whether in such sultry weather a shot bird could be kept so long.

'But we've had it buried,' she retorted in a voice edged with compassion for my ignorance. 'Put in a poc an' buried in the ground a skart will keep for weeks. Surely you knew that, mo ghaoil?'

'Oh, I knew about burying them but never more than for two or three days. I wouldn't have expected it to keep as long as this,' I replied.

'It keeps,' asserted Morag. 'An' likely it will be tender enough when we come to eat it. Did you no find yours a bitty tough on the teeths, eatin' it so soon?'

I was about to deny that I had found it tough when Flora gave me a searching look. 'Ah, but yon's gey teeth, yon,' she asserted positively. 'Yon would crack bones like a dog, yon.' She was looking at me as if she expected me to confirm her assertion.

I smiled. 'I haven't been hungry enough to try,' I told her. 'Yet,' I added.

'We'd best away for our dulse, then,' Morag said.

'Oh, stay for a cup of tea,' I urged, starting to gather up my treasury of weeds. 'I'm so dry I could drink a potful.'

'I'm as dry as a crow myself,' confessed Morag. She treated the shore to a Canute-like glance. 'The tide will keep a whiley yet, I'm thinkin'.'

'The kettles's been at the side of the fire all afternoon so it won't take long to boil,' I told her.

'Ach, then I'll away to the house an' fuse the tea while you finish your clearin'. Flora will give you a hand.'

Flora gave me a hand, accompanying her labours with such loquacious unintelligibility that I had to judge from her expression or intonation where to smile or to nod or exclaim. It appeared to suffice. As we turned to go back to the cottage she paused and with both arms full of weeds contrived to jerk an elbow towards the still unweeded part of my potato plot.

'Yon's filthy, yon,' she commented with powerful disgust. I nodded rueful agreement. It deserved no more generous a criticism.

It was good to see Morag pouring out the tea as we entered the kitchen and while I rinsed the dirt off my hands with a dipper of cold water and emptied the earth and grit out of my shoes, Morag, who was as much at home in my kitchen as her own, unwrapped the tea-towel from the girdle scones I had baked that morning, spread them with butter and jam and placed one on top of each steaming cup. In Bruach where all water had to be carried one never used more crockery than was absolutely essential. A cup required no saucer; a scone could be balanced on a cup until it was taken in the fingers. It might mean slops on the table or crumbs on the floor but rough wood is soon mopped clean and hens are good gleaners.

We sat down, Morag on a hard-backed chair near the open door so that she should not miss anything that was happening; Flora on a coir boat's fender which I had found on the shore and now used as a pouffe, and I in my usual armchair.

'Tell me, did you have yon mannie to see you?' asked Morag, slewing round in her chair.

'Was it a man?' I countered with a chuckle. 'I wasn't sure what it was.' I turned to Flora. 'This figure,' I explained, 'just came to me out of the blue and asked, "Do you love the Lord?" '

Flora brayed with laughter. 'Yon's mad, yon,' she declared.

'It was sluicing with rain,' I went on, 'and the figure was in oilskins and sou'wester and it had a high-pitched voice...'

9

'An' long hair,' interrupted Morag. 'Though the Dear only knows why a man would want to grow his hair long unless he had a disease or somethin'.'

'It was a "he", then? Are you sure?'

'Indeed, I couldn't be sure what he was myself unless I turned him upside down,' replied Morag. 'But no, mo ghaoil, that wasn't the one I was meanin'. There was another one came.'

'Was there? No, I didn't see him.'

'They were sayin' he was one of these Yanks.'

'A Yank? Oh, no, I haven't had any Americans calling on me,' I told her. 'Just the hermaphrodite.'

'Oh, is that what he was?' enquired Morag. 'I wondered what religion he had to make him grow his hair as long as that.' She threw a crumb of scone to a straying hen.

'Well, if you didn't have the Yank callin' you missed somethin', I'm tellin' you.' She wiped away a smile with the back of her hand. 'He was wearin' a kilt that near reached his ankles an' short white stockings an' a straw hat an' them dark glasses so you couldn't see if he had eyes or spider's webs behind them.'

Flora shrieked appreciation, and the laughter lines ploughed deep on Morag's wrinkled face.

'What did he want?' I asked.

'Am't I tellin' you?' reproved Morag. 'He comes to my house an' when I go to the door he asks will I take him into the cow byre an' show him my antics.'

'Your what!' I ejaculated.

'My antics,' she reiterated and seeing my expression added: 'He offered to pay me, true as I'm here.' She reached over to the table and put down her cup. 'I told him, says I, "A few years ago if you'd come then to me I could have shown you plenty of antics but ach, not now. Those days have passed." '

'What sort of antiques was he after?' I enquired soberly.

'Why, crusie lamps an' steelyards an' quern stones an' goffering irons – even the worm we had for the whisky he was wantin'.'

'I know what happened to the worm,' I said. (Morag had once told me that after receiving warning of an impending visit by the Customs man all the village's whisky-distilling apparatus had been dumped into the deepest well.) 'But did you find anything else for him?'

'I did not, then.' She rose and helped herself to another cup of tea. 'The quern stones I had right enough till Hector broke them up to use for his lobster creels, the wretch, an' the cruise lamp disappeared when he was short of somethin' to oil the engine of his boat.'

'But the goffering iron,' I reminded her. 'Your mother's goffering iron was still in the byre when I was with you. I remember your bringing it out to show me.'

Morag gave a snort of disgust. 'Indeed, mo ghaoil, but since Hector an' Behag's come to live with me what can I keep my hands on save my own breeks an' it's tight I have to hold on to them sometimes for fear Hector will snatch them for cleanin' his engine,' she complained bitterly. 'No, but didn't Behag take the gofferin' iron first for liftin' the crabs' claws out of the fire when she'd toast them – as if she couldn't do that with her fingers – an' then the next I see is Hector's got hold of it an' usin' it for stirrin' the tar to put on his boat. The Dear knows where the iron is now,' she went on. 'I doubt it's at the bottom of the sea along with the boat he tarred.'

'What a pity,' I murmured. 'I remember your telling me how you used to love watching your mother sitting by the fire and crimping the lace on her bonnet with the hot iron.'

Morag stared reflectively through the doorway, a gentle smile hovering around her lips. 'Indeed, I remember it like yesterday,' she said with a wistful sigh.

11

Down on the shore Morag and Flora wrested brown dulse from the wet, limpet-stippled rocks until their bag was full when they came up to the tide's edge and joined me in the collection of driftwood. No matter how adequate one's store of driftwood might be it was impossible to resist taking home bundle after bundle rather than leave it for the tide to take away again. Morag looked up at the sky, assessing the degree of light.

'If we don't start back they'll be thinkin' the "Each Uisge" has got us,' said Morag. 'An' there'll be no milk for the tea if I don't away to the cow. Hector's awful heavy on the milk,' she explained.

We made our way towards the heather-fringed burn where a relatively easy path led up towards the crofts. By now it was time for the evening milking and we could hear, though we could not yet see, the milkers calling for their cattle over the echoing moors. From closer at hand came the bawling of frustrated calves which, recognising the calling and the clanging of milk pails as a portent of supper, would be cavorting within the limited circle of their tethers.

Beside the burn Erchy was working at his dinghy, gouging handfuls of thick yellow grease from a tin he had found washed up on the shore and ramming it between the gaping planks. Like all Bruachites he had a sublime faith in grease and tar for keeping out the sea.

'Are you gettin' good fishin'?' enquired Morag, surveying with unusual interest the floorboards of the dinghy which were speckled with fish scales.

'Aye. There's plenty of fish about now,' he admitted.

'The sea's hissin' with mackerel.' With his elbow he gestured towards the outlying islands. 'There's a bit of herrin' too. Tearlaich an' me, we brought home a nice few herrin' last night.' He and Morag exchanged wary glances.

12

Flora, still carrying her bundle of wood, leaned over the boat. 'Yon's no herrin' scales, yon,' she stated flatly. 'No, nor mackerel either.'

'Indeed they are so,' argued Erchy but with dwindling defiance as he realised he was confronted by an expert. He glanced again at Morag but she had turned away, elaborately disinterested.

'Yon's salmon, yon!' accused Flora.

'Be quiet!' returned Erchy with a challenging gleam in his eye but seeing Flora's conspiratorial smile he went on: 'What if they are salmon, anyway? It's pleased enough you'd be if you found one waitin' for you in the mornin', I doubt.'

'I would too,' agreed Flora with unusual lucidity. 'There's nay harm in yon.'

'The Lord puts the salmon in the rivers like he puts the berries on the trees,' said Morag piously. 'They're there for all of us, no' just the laird.'

'Aye so,' concurred Flora and she might just as well have said 'Amen'.

I did not need to express an opinion, having lived long enough in Bruach to accept that poaching was not just a means of obtaining trout or salmon for a tasty meal but a daring and exciting pastime. To outwit the watchers or evade the police was a game as compulsive as betting or gambling might be to a townsman, with the added attraction that it yielded a repertoire of adventure and escape stories for the participants to narrate at winter ceilidhs. Nearly every able-bodied male in the village, whatever his occupation, poached or had poached at some time or another. Even the salmon watchers were reputed to engage in a little poaching when they were not on duty.

Sure of his audience's wholehearted support Erchy became expansive. 'Indeed I mind the old laird askin' me to poach his salmon for him more than once,' he told us.

'Go on!' taunted Flora.

'Damty sure he did. I was doin' watchin' for him then an' he was expectin' this house party to come an' wanted salmon for their dinner. He was up at the loch all day an' didn't get a bite so he comes to me an' he says till I put my net in the river that night an' make sure there'd be one or two nice fish for them.'

'An' you made sure,' put in Morag with a reminiscent smile.

'Aye, we got near a dozen so we picked out all the ones that had the marks of the net on them an' sent them up to the laird's house. The rest we kept for ourselves.'

'That wasn't right at all,' Morag chided him.

'Ach, the cook got a hold of them an' had them prepared before the guests could put an eye to them but the next time the laird asks me to poach a few for him he says, "An' mind you, Erchy, make sure there's no net marks on them this time. I cannot rely on this cook to make such a good job of them." '

'Is it true?' demanded Flora.

'As true as I'm here,' averred Erchy.

Flora shook her head. 'Yon's a mon, yon.'

'These are no' very fresh,' Morag declared, leaning over the boat and scraping at the scales adhering to the wood. 'Would these be the minister's scales?'

Flora and I exchanged amused glances. 'The minister's scales?' we said simultaneously.

'What I was meanin' was were they the scales left from the night he had the minister out poachin'.' She laughed. 'The night Erchy spent in the gaol.'

'Never surely!' breathed Flora.

'Aye, we did,' Erchy confirmed. 'Him as well.'

'The minister?'

'Aye.' Erchy nodded smugly. 'An' it served him damty well right too.'

'What happened?' I asked.

'Well, you mind that Sassenach minister was over stayin' for a holiday last week?'

I nodded.

'Well him, it was. He mentioned more than once he'd like a nice salmon to take back with him so in the end I said I'd take him. We went to the river an' we'd got a couple of good salmon in the net when suddenly there's a shout an' a couple of pollis come out of the dark an' grab the net, salmon an' all. They couldn't see who we was an' I got away out of it quick but this daft minister shouts, "No, Erchy, it's no use. We're caught red-handed." God! I was that mad I could have hit him. If he'd had any sense he would have followed me an' they'd never have been able to prove it was our net. We could always have said we'd just noticed it there an' were havin' a look.'

'You'd have lost your net,' I pointed out.

'We could have got a new bit of net for the price of the fine,' returned Erchy.

'So they put you in gaol,' I sympathised.

'Aye, well, that fellow wouldn't be satisfied. "We must plead guilty, Erchy," he says to me. "No damty fear," says I. "They've no proof, I tell you." "But, Erchy," says he, "if there's a case about it my name will be in the papers an' what will my congregation think if they see their minister's been caught poachin'?" '

'The man was right,' interrupted Morag. 'He has to think of his congregation.'

'Right for himself maybe but ministers should think about others as well,' returned Erchy. 'If he was goin' to plead guilty then I had to as well.'

'What difference does it make pleading guilty?' I enquired innocently.

'If you plead guilty you just spend the night in the cell an' in the mornin' you pay your fine an' get out an' nobody much the wiser,' he explained.

'So that's what they did. An' the minister didn't get his salmon to take back with him,' Morag said.

'No, but he had the cheek of the devil, that fellow,' Erchy disclosed. 'When the copper came to the cell the next mornin' he was mighty pleased with himself at havin' got the pair of us an' the two salmon as evidence. Oh, he was smilin' an' tellin' us it was a nice day, an' then he says, "What would you like for your breakfast, gentlemen?" as if it was a hotel we was stayin' at.

' "I fancy some bacon an' eggs," says I, thinkin' I'd be cheeky an' put them to as much trouble as I could.

' "An' what about you, minister?" he says. An' that minister looks at him as cool as I don't know what an' he says, "Oh, don't go to any trouble for me, boys, just give me the same as you had yourselves – a plate of poached salmon".'

Flora and I dissolved into laughter.

'We'd best be on our way,' said Morag. 'Oidhche mhath!' she called.

'Oidhche mhath!' responded Erchy. I had taken a couple of steps in the wake of Morag and Flora when I realised that Erchy's farewell had been spoken with his normal clarity and I realised suddenly that he was equipped with a full set of teeth.

'Erchy!' I exclaimed, instantly recognising them as his own because of the broken eye tooth. 'You've got your teeth back again!'

'Aye, I have so,' he admitted.

'You were lucky to find them, weren't you? Didn't you tell me you dropped them in the sea?'

'I said I dropped them overboard,' corrected Erchy, and seeing my puzzled look elucidated: 'I dropped them overboard in the river the other night when I was poachin' an' I was certain I'd never see them again, but, aye, I was lucky. Somebody did find them. They got them in their net.'

'How extraordinary!' I said. 'Who got them?'

'I'm not sayin' who,' responded Erchy with an air of mystery, 'but this mornin' who should be at the door but the pollis an' when I asked him what he wanted he pulled out this handkerchief an' there was my teeths wrapped in it. "I hear you lost your teeths, Erchy," says he. "Well, I did so," says I. "I'm wonderin' if these are yours?" asks the pollis. Well, I knew fine anybody would know they're my teeths so I says, "Aye, they're mine, right enough."'

'But who would take them to the police?' I asked. 'Surely it would be tantamount to admitting they'd been poaching?'

'Who would take them to the pollis?' returned Erchy derisively. 'When I'm damty sure everyone in the village knew they was mine?'

'You mean...' I began and then paused as the full import of his words dawned slowly upon me. 'You mean the policeman himself was doing a spot of poaching and he caught them in his net?'

Erchy fixed me with an uncompromising stare. 'Now what damty fool would be askin' the pollis a question like that?' he demanded.

Hic Jacet!

Erchy's mother and I met down by the burn where I had been looking for watercress and when I had first spotted her standing barefoot in the peaty brown pool below the waterfall I stood captivated by the picture she made. With sleeves rolled elbow high and skirts tucked well above the knees she was carefully positioning two empty herring barrels beneath a craggy rock over which a truant rivulet of sparkling water poured gently enough to fill the barrels without risk of bursting them. Satisfied at last she waded about in the pool, selecting boulders to buttress the barrels until finally, after a push or two to assure herself of their rigidity, she waded back to the bank where she stood for a moment assessing her handiwork while she shook stray drops of water from her cotton bonnet. I marvelled at her toughness. Erchy's mother was 'Seventy past'; I knew from experience how bitingly cold the water in the pool felt to bare feet even in midsummer and guessed she had been enduring it for at least ten minutes. I continued watching while she sat on the heathery bank, drying her feet on her long skirts, pulling on a pair of thick black woollen stockings to just above the knee and finally lacing up her sturdy 'tackety' boots. Not until then did I make my presence known.

'He Breeah!'

'He Breeah!' She struggled up. 'Were you here long?'

'Oh, no,' I lied, fearing to embarrass her. 'I've just been making my way along the burn.' I showed her my few sprigs of watercress.

'Ach, the biolaire, as we have it in the Gaelic,' she commented and with a smile added, 'that's food for the wee folk.'

'I've heard that.' I returned her smile.

'Aye, there's some folks hereabouts who'll swear to seein' a wee mannie gatherin' it late at night but only the Dear knows whether or not they were tellin' the truth.'

'I'm very fond of it,' I told her.

'Aye, an' so were some of the laird's folk in my mother's day, I mind her tellin' me. But she had no likin' for it herself an' I daresay that's why I've never taken to it.' She tucked stray wisps of white hair into her bonnet and tied the strings under her chin. Waking or sleeping Erchy's mother rarely left her head uncovered. Most of the year she wore knitted woollen helmets but on hot summer days it was always the old-fashioned but extremely becoming cotton bonnet.

'Seein' you're here you'll came an' take a wee strupach with me,' she informed me. 'It's an awful whiley since you were in my house.'

Already I had been out longer than I had intended but to have refused her invitation would have disconcerted us both. She turned to take a last glance at the two barrels now full and overflowing.

'How long will you leave them there?' I asked.

'Till Friday maybe,' she replied.

It was now Tuesday and I estimated that three full days under the waterfall would have cleaned the barrels better than any amount of scrubbing or scouring. To Bruachites whose homes were nearby the burn became merely an extension of their kitchens. There on the bank, supported by a couple of fire-blackened rocks and permanently in

19

residence, Erchy's mother kept a large iron washing pot in which she boiled her linen, rinsing it afterwards in the fast-flowing burn; it was in the burn she did her annual blanket washing prior to draping them over high clumps of heather to dry in the sun. There she cleaned the insides of the sheep they killed each autumn and there she washed the meal-coated bowls and basins when she had finished baking.

As we drew near the cottage she shielded her eyes from the sun. 'There's the men busy at their bottoms,' she observed.

At the gable end of the house Erchy was thrusting a rusty gap-toothed saw through a plank of driftwood with the object of cutting it into lengths suitable for bottoms for lobster creels. The saw scrunched and jammed, scrunched and jammed again and again and Erchy swore and jounced, swore and jounced in retaliation. Nearby crouched Hector, chewing at a stalk of grass and watching the proceedings with cursory interest.

'I'm after tellin' Erchy he needs to take tsat saw to see a dentist,' he quipped as we paused to watch.

The saw, Erchy and his profanity jerked to a stop as he looked up. His face was red as a radish with exertion and a large bead of sweat dropped from his upper lip as he nodded acknowledgment of our presence.

'Indeed I'm thinkin' I could chew through it faster,' he confessed, dragging a tired arm across his glistening brow and giving the saw a long look of disgust. It was rare to see a well-kept tool in Bruach and it struck me that Erchy might have sawn wood more efficiently with a curry comb.

'It wouldn't be so bad if that bugger would take his turn at it.' Erchy nodded cheerfully at Hector.

'Ach, I'm no good wiss a saw,' Hector disclaimed hastily and giving Erchy a respectful look went on: 'Erchy's tsat

20

good at it I believe if he had a mind he could make coffins as good as any undertaker.'

'I'll make one for you,' retorted Erchy searingly. 'An' I'll make it good an' strong. That's one job you won't wriggle out of.'

Hector smiled imperturbably. He turned to me. 'Me an' Erchy has a mind to go to Rhuna tsis evenin',' he disclosed. 'She'll stay calm enough, I reckon.' He stared with indolent optimism at the sunlit sea, frisked into sharp-edged ripples by a tease of afternoon breeze.

Erchy's mother turned on her son with mock indignation.

'How can you be goin' away to Rhuna when only this mornin' you were sayin' you hadn't the time to take from makin' the creels to bring home a load of peats just.'

'An' isn't it for the sake of the creels we have to go to Rhuna?' he exclaimed, glancing quickly at Hector, inviting endorsement of his statement. Hector's wide-eyed assent was very convincing.

'Ach!' The old woman's tone was explicit.

'It's true,' Erchy insisted. 'We need to go an' gather up the hazels we cut earlier this year. You canna make creels without hazels any more than you can make bannocks without meal.'

'I can see I'll be needin' to take home the peats myself, then,' his mother said with pretended resignation as she flexed her shoulders proudly.

'Aye, you will so,' agreed her son.

It seemed never to have occurred to Erchy and it would have been cruel to suggest to his mother that she was now too old to carry home heavy creels of peat from the moors. She had carried them since childhood and through the years her back had shaped itself to take the half-hundredweight or so of the loaded creels. Like her contemporaries she would continue to do so, insisting that stiff fingers could still grasp peats and a back rigid with rheumatism was still sound enough for burdens. Not until the day came when with only a token load of peats and making frequent stops for rest she found herself too breathless to totter to and from the moors would she give in. With a grunt that was acceptance of her son's remark and a warm 'thig a 's Tigh' to me she made for the cottage. However, I hung back for a moment.

'Does this trip to Rhuna mean there's likely to be a cruise?' I asked, looking appreciatively at the roan-coloured islands. 'It promises to be a perfect evening for a sail.'

'The sea makes no promises and breaks none,' Erchy rebuked me.

Hector contemplated his chewed stalk of grass, discarded it and chose another one. 'We're no likely to get away by ourselves, anyway,' he remarked philosophically. 'Tsere's always plenty folks keen enough to go to Rhuna on a nice evenin'. I daresay we'll get enough to sink tse boat.'

'I'll look out for you then?' I suggested.

'Aye, you'd best do that if you're comin',' said Erchy. 'At the back of eight or so.' He bent to resume his contest with the saw.

In the kitchen Erchy's mother was unwrapping crumbly oatcakes from a piece of bleached flour sack which in Bruach kitchens did duty as tea-towels. 'They're fresh-baked this mornin' an' left warm beside the fire,' she told me. In my larder at home were fresh mackerel fillets waiting only to be dipped in oatmeal and baked for my supper and I had eaten frugally all day so as to be able to indulge in what had now become my favourite dish. But Erchy's mother baked the most irresistible oatcakes in Bruach and I knew without doubt I should succumb. She cut a thick slice of home-made butter and placing it on the triangular cake offered it to me. In the Bruach idiom 'my teeths watered' as I watched the butter melting into a golden lake.

There was a footstep outside followed by a Gaelic greeting. I recognised Morag's voice.

'Ach, so this is where you are!' she said, coming inside and settling herself ready for the strupak which Erchy's mother immediately prepared for her.

I wiped the butter from my chin. 'Why, were you looking for me?' I asked.

'No, but seein' I was up at the Post Office Behag said would I call in an' tell you she'll likely be down for a wee ceilidh with you tonight. She sent away to the catalogue for a new skirt an' she's wantin' you to gather her in round the middle.'

'Not tonight,' I said. 'There's going to be a cruise. Have you not heard?'

'A cruise!' she ejaculated. 'What way are you goin'?'

'To Rhuna,' I replied. 'Hector and Erchy have to go over to collect some hazels to finish their creels.'

'If that's the way of it, mo ghaoil, I doubt you'll be seein' Behag tonight except on the boat beside you,' Morag said. 'An' myself too, likely,' she added. 'I haven't set foot on Rhuna these ten years since.'

'I was with you myself last time you were there, was I not?' Erchy's mother reminded her.

'You were so,' Morag acknowledged.

'That man Hamish Beag was alive then. You mind the one that played the bagpipes and wouldn't speak to a soul save his horse.'

Morag nodded.

'He played his bagpipes the night we was there,' Erchy's mother recalled.

'Indeed, that's true,' returned Morag. She turned to me. 'I'm tellin' you, Miss Peckwitt, that man stood in the door of his house an' the minute he started to play his pipes all the rats ran out an' hid themselves they was that feared of the noise.' The two women chuckled reminiscently.

'They say he was forever blowin' his bagpipes,' said Erchy's mother.

'An' they were right. That's what folks say killed him in the end,' Morag told us.

'Not playing the bagpipes?' I protested.

'So they say.' Morag nodded slowly. 'Insanity of the lungs, that's what he got with playin' the pipes so much, mo ghaoil, an' that's what killed him in the end.'

'Is there a strupach, cailleach?' Erchy sauntered into the kitchen followed by Hector and in their wake came Tearlaich who was carrying a slightly less disabled saw than the one Erchy had been using. Morag shot Tearlaich a disapproving glance. He was something of a non-conformist in Bruach and he came in now with his jacket slung over his shoulder and his shirt open to the waist revealing a fuzzy chest as broad and muscular as that of a champion plough horse.

'Are you no goin' to fasten up your shirt seein' there's ladies present,' she said to him, half jokingly. Tearlaich responded with a brazen smile but nevertheless began to do up his shirt buttons.

Erchy's mother's eyes grew bright with pleasure as her kitchen filled and she busied herself buttering oatcakes and pouring cups of tea. 'If the cows hadn't yet to be milked we could have a ceilidh,' she said wistfully.

The three men flopped down on the bench. I was sitting on an uneven stool and as I raised my overfull teacup to drink the stool wobbled and the hot tea slopped into my lap. I let out a startled exclamation and began mopping myself with a handkerchief. Tearlaich, who claimed to have acted as batman to a high-ranking officer during the war and who still retained a desultory interest in chivalry, immediately jumped up.

'What are we doing taking the best seats for ourselves,' he chided himself and the others. 'Come now, Miss Peckwitt, and take my seat and I will have that old stool,' he offered gallantly. Erchy and Hector flicked him the sort of glance that would have been merited by a potato that showed signs of blight.

'That's not goin' to do her any harm at her age,' Erchy said pitilessly.

I refused to give up my stool, knowing that if I sat near them neither Erchy nor Hector would be able to resist indulging in the time-honoured trick of leaving a teaspoon in their tea until it was really hot, then whipping it out and pressing it on to my bare arm. Tearlaich promptly resumed his seat on the bench. He offered his saw to Erchy.

'Here,' he said. 'Take a lend of this.'

Erchy took it without enthusiasm at first but then examining the handle more closely he exclaimed: 'Here, this is my own saw! I know him by these three cuts on the handle.'

Tearlaich leaned over to inspect the notches. 'Aye,' he allowed. 'It's marked all right.'

'Where did you get him from then?' Erchy demanded.

'From Johnny Mor Alistair.'

'Oh, that bugger!' commented Erchy, without venom.

His mother darted him a reproving glance. No matter how much evidence she heard to the contrary she would undoubtedly go to her grave still cherishing the belief that her son never swore except in Gaelic.

'No wonder he didn't mind me gettin' the lend of it for you,' Tearlaich mused.

'Hell, no! But it wasn't Johnny Mor Alistair that took him from me in the first place. I believe it was Lachlan Beag that had him to make his wee hoosie when his brother was comin' home an' bringin' that fancy girl friend of his.'

'Oh, her,' responded Tearlaich derisively. 'The one that was too swanky to use the heather like the rest of us.' He grunted. 'It's a good thing he didn't marry that one. If she had to have a wee hoosie before she'd marry him God knows what she would have been askin' for next.'

'One of them Rolls-Royces to carry home the peats, likely,' submitted Hector with a smile.

Erchy still held the saw. 'He was a good saw when he was new,' he murmured sadly.

'Did you get it new?' asked Tearlaich incredulously.

'No, but my father did,' replied Erchy. 'He got him from the blacksmith after he died.'

'But the blacksmith died twenty years since,' Tearlaich expostulated.

'Aye, an' he was as good as new then.' Erchy ran his fingers along the toothed edge. 'He's still better than that one I was usin', anyway.' He put the saw on the floor under the bench. 'I'd like to know who Johnny Mor Alistair got him from all the same.'

'Who knows where any of the tools in this place comes from,' retorted Tearlaich, adding as an afterthought, 'From hell itself by the look of most of them.'

He took out a packet of cigarettes and extracting four pushed one behind his ear, gave one to Erchy, one to Hector and was about to bestow the fourth one on me when he suddenly changed his mind and pushed it back into the packet which he then held out to me. 'Sao,' he invited politely.

Hector stretched out his hand and helped himself to a piece of oatcake from the table. 'Indeed amn't I wishin' Behag could make tsem as good as tsese,' he said plaintively.

'Ach, but she was never born to it,' Morag defended. Behag's parents had both been crofters but as they were never married Behag herself had been adopted by a

26

Glasgow couple and had visited Bruach only for occasional holidays until she met and married Hector.

'It's funny that,' observed Erchy with a puzzled frown.

'What's funny?' asked Hector.

'The way Behag was adopted. You'd think with her mother bein' from Bruach her own parents would have kept the child and been glad to do it.'

'It's always struck me as odd,' I interposed. I had lived there long enough now to know that any child born in Bruach was sure of a welcome.

'Indeed her mother's parents wanted her to keep the child!' exclaimed Morag indignantly. 'But Kate, that was Behag's mother, thought she could do better.'

'What happened, then?' I asked.

'It was like this, mo ghaoil,' began Morag. 'When Behag was no more than about two years old her mother went off to work in Glasgow an' she went an' got herself married to a man that lived in a nice house an' seemed to have plenty of money. He lived with his parents an' was brought up one of these Papists but ach, I suppose they were gettin' old so they made no fuss about havin' a nice girl like Kate to look after them in spite of her havin' a different religion. The husband must have been a decent man for all that, for he made no objection to Kate havin' Behag to live with them an' so they were all set up until he goes an' dies on them suddenly.'

'He was very smart about his dyin', I mind,' interpolated Erchy's mother.

'Smart!' echoed Morag. 'Indeed he was. He didn't have time to do whatever it is these Papists do before they die anyway, so Kate told me.'

'What happened to Kate then?' enquired Erchy.

'Didn't the daughter come home from abroad when her brother died an' say she'd look after the old folk now, an'

Kate was told plainly either she'd change her religion or she'd get out an' take Behag with her.'

'The house an' the money belonged to the old folk all the time seemingly,' supplied Erchy's mother. 'Kate got nothin' but a few pounds out of it for all her work.'

'Did Kate get out?' I asked.

'She got out,' declared Hector grimly.

'Surely she got out.' Morag's tone made it plain there had been no alternative for a girl born and bred in Bruach. 'But Kate's parents were both dead by that time an' only her brother an' his wife in the croft. She didn't think much of the brother's wife so she had to take work herself an' get Behag adopted. It was lucky she did for she died soon after.' Morag shook her head. 'She had a sad life in a way, did Behag's mother. A sad life an' a short one.'

'This couple that adopted Behag,' pursued Erchy. 'Were they good to her?'

'Good enough,' said Hector.

'Why did they take her?' asked Tearlaich. 'Was it because they couldn't have bairns of their own?'

'Well, of course,' began Morag but Erchy cut her short.

'There's no of course about it,' he told her. 'Some of these folks that adopt children do it because they get paid more for havin' an adopted child than if it was one of their own.'

'That's true,' conceded Morag.

'An' that's as it should be,' put in Tearlaich. 'You'd expect to be paid more. After all if you've made your children you've had the fun as well.'

'Whisht now!' commanded Erchy's mother, with a glance at me.

'The shame about Behag is that she hasn't the Gaelic,' said Erchy, changing the subject.

'I don't care about her havin' tse Gaelic,' Hector responded. 'I can as well make her understand what I want of her in English as in Gaelic, but all the same I wish she could learn to make oatcakes as good as these.' He broke off a large piece and stuffed it into his mouth.

'She tries,' Morag told him.

'Aye, she tries. But you know yourself tse ones she makes are tsat bitty most of them drops on the floor for tse hens to eat.'

'Us girls had to learn,' Erchy's mother told him. 'If we wasted oatmeal it was our job to grind more on the quern stones an' that was hard work.' Leaning over the table and clasping her hands round an imaginary stick she strained, miming vividly the action of grinding the oats between the circular stones and her face became set into lines of remembered effort. She relaxed with a smile. 'How I hated havin' to do it,' she said.

'But the smell of it!' Morag reminded her. 'Did ever meal smell so good? Not like this stuff we get already ground these days.'

'To my mind nothin' smells as good these days as it once did,' Erchy's mother rejoined. 'I remember when I was young the way the flowers threw up their scent at you as you walked through the grass in the spring an' summer. An' in the autumn the tang of the heather would drift in of an evenin' over the crofts like a scented shawl.'

'An' the burn in spate,' Morag recalled. 'Once you turned your back on the sea you could smell the burn as surely as a fox smells a new lamb from afar off.'

'An' the honey! D'you mind the honey?' exclaimed Erchy's mother, her eyes glowing with reminiscence. 'The way it was that strong you could fairly taste the sweetness of it on your lips as you walked in the heather.'

'Aye, an' the hems of your skirt would be sticky with it when you came to take off your clothes at night.'

'It's funny you never smell such things now,' went on Erchy's mother. 'It's like as though the lovely smells of the place had been washed away with all the rain that's in it.'

'You're right,' agreed Morag. 'I've noticed that myself.'

Erchy seemed to be growing more and more uneasy as the recollections continued. 'Of course everythin' smells the same, you silly cailleachs,' he broke in. 'It's just you two gettin' old that's the trouble.'

Morag looked momentarily stricken but his mother smiled confidently. 'My nose is still above the ground,' she told him as she gathered up the cloth in which the oatcakes had been wrapped. Going to the doorway she flicked off the crumbs to a waiting cluster of hens.

'The trouble with the cailleach is she won't allow anybody to be old so long as they can stand on their own two feets just,' Erchy muttered with kindly understanding.

'When I was a girl,' said Erchy's mother as she came back into the kitchen, 'there was little ground oatmeal came into our house.'

Erchy fished a half-smoked cigarette from his trouser pocket and lit it. 'I mind my father bringing home meal that was already ground,' he said.

'Aye, but those were bad days indeed.' His mother's voice was unusually sharp.

I looked enquiringly from mother to son, sensing a story. 'How bad?' I asked.

'Ach, it was the laird that was here at the time. He was a bad man, Miss Peckwitt. A bad man indeed.' She took the kettle over to the water pail and refilled it.

'You'd best finish tellin' her now you've started,' Erchy encouraged her.

'Since you remember it you can tell her yourself,' his mother retorted.

'Ach, I was young at the time. I only mind my father tellin' me of it.'

'He'd be tellin' you the truth, then, so you can tell Miss Peckwitt the truth now.'

Contentedly Erchy embarked on his narrative. 'It was like my mother said. This laird that was here then was a hard man. A cruel man you could say an' when he wanted work doin' on the estate he'd drive round Bruach in his pony an' trap an' any man he'd put an eye on he'd point his whip at him an' say, "I've seen you." He never said a word more than "I've seen you" but once he'd pointed at the men then those men had to go the next day an' do a day's work for him. It didn't matter how much work they needed to do on their own crofts – they might have oats or hay to stack an' the weather like to break at any moment, but they had to leave it an' go at first light the next day to the laird's place and work right through till it was dark. All they got in payment was a measure of meal. Just that. No money.'

'But it was the measure that was wicked,' interrupted his mother.

'I was comin' to that,' he told her. 'This measure he had was a bit like a small herrin' barrel but it was divided into two across the middle.' He got up and going across to the dresser picked up an old-fashioned wooden egg-cup. 'The shape of it was a bit like this only bigger an' with this sort of waist in it so that the top half held a lot more meal than the bottom half. When the work was finished for the day the laird would make the men stand in two lines, the big men in one line an' the small ones in the other. They'd hold out their pocs an' the big men would get the big measure of meal tipped into it an' the small men would get the small measure.'

'All for the same day's work?' I asked.

'For the same day's work,' confirmed Erchy.

'What if the big man was a bachelor and the small man had a family to keep?' I pursued.

'Then that was the way of it,' was the reply. 'That's how they were paid no matter what family they had.'

It all sounded so medieval that I looked askance at Erchy, recalling that his father had still been alive when I had first come to Bruach.

'And all this happened in your father's time?' I could not keep the incredulity out of my voice.

'Aye. An' I mind it happenin', though I was young enough at the time.'

'Aye, he was young enough,' affirmed his mother. 'But if he didn't remember it he'd have heard the men speakin' of it for that they did often enough. They miscalled that man somethin' terrible, Miss Peckwitt, an' he deserved every bit of it.'

'And did this continue until the new laird took over?' I demanded, knowing that the crofters were eager enough now to be given work on the estate.

'It did not then.' Erchy's denial held a note of triumph. 'It was Big Ruari that put a stop to it.'

'Big Ruari?' I echoed. 'You mean...?'

'No, not the Big Ruari that's alive today but his uncle,' Erchy corrected. 'He got the men together one day an' told them if they'd all stick by him they need never again work for the laird except for money or fair shares.'

'Big Ruari was my own father's cousin,' mused Hector.

'He was my own husband's cousin at that,' claimed Erchy's mother proudly.

'Wasn't he marrit to Anna Ruag that was an aunt of mine,' asserted Morag.

As everyone in Bruach appeared to be related in some degree or other to everyone else I saw there was a danger that the story of Big Ruari's stratagem for overcoming the laird might be relinquished in favour of a prolonged delving into genealogies, so after a few minutes of simulated attention I put my question direct. 'How did Big Ruari stop them working for the laird?'

There was a hint of recoil and in the ensuing silence Erchy got up and made me wait while he searched in a drawer of the dresser for a crumpled packet of cigarettes. Outside two cockerels began to crow competitively.

'Well,' resumed Erchy, sitting down. 'The men was all agreed that next time the laird was seen comin' in his trap they'd make themselves scarce except for Big Ruari an' he'd stay workin' near the road so the laird couldn't help seein' him. Right enough, along comes the laird, points his whip at Big Ruari an' says, "I've seen you." Big Ruari touched his cap as he was supposed to but he didn't turn up for work the next day, no, nor the next. Back comes the laird an' by God! he's mad. There's Big Ruari again workin' beside the road but the rest of the men is hidden in his byre. "Why did you not come to do your day's work like you were told?" roars the laird. "See you come tomorrow, my man, or it'll be the worse for you." "I'm no' coming to work for you tomorrow nor any other day," Big Ruari tells him. "An' what's more there's no man in this place will ever work for you again except for fair wages." As soon as Big Ruari's done speakin' the laird ups with his whip an' gives him a mighty strike across the face so that the blood comes pouring out.'

'Oh, but he was a monster, that laird!' interjected Erchy's mother. 'An' him a Highlander!'

'Aye, he was so,' affirmed Erchy, gesturing his mother to remain silent. 'Big Ruari then, he steps up to the trap. "In that case, master, I'll do my day's work now," says he, an' he lifts the laird clean out of the trap an' throws him down on the ground. Then the rest of the men rushes out, unhitches the horse and send it harin' away for home. They turn the trap right over on top of the laird so that it's like he's caught in a cage. An' there they left him an' went back to their own croft work.'

'An' no Bruach man ever did a day's work for that laird again,' said Morag dramatically.

'I suppose he sold up and left eventually,' I suggested, recalling that the only lairds I had heard spoken of had been Lowlanders.

'He did not, then. He died here in his own house,' Erchy refuted. 'Isn't that his grave in the woods you were askin' about yourself a good while back?'

'Oh, that's his grave, is it?' I said thoughtfully, and was glad that at last I had discovered the story of the lone grave. I had come upon it suddenly while blackberrying in a gentle birchwood not far from the laird's house. The surrounding iron railings had fallen outwards and were partially embedded in the moist earth but the area of the grave was still clearly marked by an abundant growth of nettles impressively green in contrast with the pale spongy moss elsewhere; the roots of a young tree had shattered what must once have been a large headstone. I had not lived long in Bruach when I had made my find and doubtless I had asked too many questions for a stranger so that when I had enquired about the lone grave I had been told merely that its occupant had been a Roman Catholic and therefore could not be buried in the Bruach burial ground. Instinctively I had suspected more of a story but I had had to wait several years to hear it fully.

'Aye, that's his grave,' Tearlaich agreed. 'And I'm telling you, Miss Peckwitt, that laird was so much hated, if any man from Bruach needed to have a pee and he was within a mile of that wood he'd hold on to himself till he could get there just so he could have the pleasure of defiling that grave.'

'Indeed I do it myself to this day,' boasted Erchy.

'Be quiet!' his mother admonished him. 'Miss Peckwitt won't like to hear you.'

I laughed heartily. 'I wondered why those nettles look so well fertilised,' I said.

In Search of Apples

It was well after the 'back of eight' before the first potential passengers began to drift in twos and threes down to the shore but since there was no sign of either Erchy or Hector I occupied myself with tidying up the tiny flower garden behind my cottage while keeping an eye open for signs of activity aboard the boat. My garden had perforce to be a tiny one since in Bruach adequate shelter had to be provided from the savage storms which constantly beset us irrespective of the time of year. The only satisfactory shelter was a dry-stone wall, the building of which is infinitely more complicated than it appears and though initially I had planned a garden large enough to grow shrubs and roses as well as annuals, as I had wrestled throughout the winter months with craggy jumbo-sized stones that perversely slid from their beds as soon as my back was turned so had my plans contracted until finally I was more than content with a plot that measured little more than three strides by two. I was able to rejoice that I had some shelter and when spring came I sowed the garden prodigally with seed that the catalogues described as being 'the hardiest of hardy annuals': marigolds, poppies, candy-tuft, lavatera, and flax among them. I had tried to sow to a preconceived pattern of colour but when the seedlings appeared they did so in haphazard swirls acknowledging the eddies of a vagrant breeze that had been loitering, too stealthily for my wind-conditioned body to notice, around the garden at the time of sowing. The seedlings had flourished and now after a few days of calm and sunshine the full-grown plants were exploding into bloom, making a patch of colour on the drab croft like a brightly crocheted cushion in a barren room. I sometimes asked myself why I so much wanted a flower garden when, in their season, there was such an abundance of wild flowers to delight the eye. Celandines, primroses, red rattle, butterwort, St John's wort, corn marigold, orchis and countless other gems studded the crofts and moors with their discreet beauty until eclipsed by the autumnal glory of the heather, but comely as they were they were all either tiny or tough-stemmed plants and perversely I found myself missing the long-stemmed elegance of garden flowers. I stood regarding my plot, revelling in its colour and dwelling on even more ambitious plans. A rose bush here – my eye marked the spot. And another one there...

'Them's bloody lovely,' said an unctuous voice in my ear and I turned to see Tearlaich who had come up quietly behind me and was regarding the flowers with eye-bulging admiration. 'Bloody lovely!' he confirmed with a congratulatory nod. Tearlaich was convinced that he possessed a rare eye for beauty. 'I'd like to grow flowers myself,' he confided. 'Indeed I did try to grow some once or twice just to see what they'd look like.'

'And were you successful?' I asked.

'Ach! It was always the same. Either the cows got at them or the sheep ate them or the horses broke down the fence and let the hens into them.'

I sympathised with him. There was little enough encouragement for would-be gardeners, particularly flower gardeners, in Bruach, since even in summer with the moor gates closed against the cattle there were always straying animals eager to devastate any unfenced crops and traditionally once the hay and corn and potatoes were lifted and stacked the gates were thrown open again allowing the voracious cattle to rampage in and feast on the aftermath of grass. During their first few days on the crofts the air was filled with the noise of clashing horns, thumping bodies and bellows of aggression or agony as the half-wild cattle which had all summer been free to wander over the vast expanse of moorlands found themselves confined within the relatively small area of croftland and we, their owners, went about our daily chores with anxious eyes ranging over the cliffs and gullies near the shore and carrying hefty sticks ready to drive a beast away from danger or break up what might prove to be a disastrous encounter for one's own or someone else's cow. By the time the herds had amalgamated and were concentrating on feeding rather than fighting the crofts had been churned into morasses of mud by their hooves and only the most robust fences had withstood their blundering assaults.

I was fortunate in that my cottage and byre were enclosed by a sturdy dry-stone wall, or dyke as it was always called in Bruach, which so long as I assiduously replaced any fallen stones was an effective barrier against the cows while the horses, which were not allowed on the crofts until the cows had gleaned most of the grass, were too busy seeking for food to have the energy for anything but dragging themselves from one promising-looking patch to another. My henhouse was far enough away to discourage the poultry from too close an investigation of the cottage and its immediate surroundings but it was the sheep which were my enemies. Against these I had little defence save sharp eyes, a supply of small stones and a stentorian repetition of 'Halla!' whenever they came in sight.

'It's a pity there aren't more gardens in Bruach,' I observed to Tearlaich. 'If more people grew vegetables or flowers they might be keener to keep the cattle away from the crofts at night.' It was difficult enough maintaining a watch on one's garden during daylight: it was virtually impossible to do so once darkness had fallen.

'Ach, but there's always the slugs to spoil a garden,' responded Tearlaich nimbly. 'It's that damp on my croft the slugs are near as big as mice. I grew some cabbages last year and I could lie in my bed at night and listen to the slugs gnawing through them.'

I laughed.

'It's as true as I'm here,' he assured me with great earnestness. 'Honest to God, those cabbages were as full of holes as a herring net by morning.'

From the shore came the rattle of oars being shipped.

'Have Erchy and Hector gone down yet?' I asked.

'Aye, they're away. They told me to call in and tell you to be ready and for me to pick up that rope fender Erchy dropped over your dyke a while back.'

My croft being situated conveniently near was the repository for precious objects retrieved from the shore. There were times after a storm when my croft resembled a museum of flotsam.

'I'll go and get a coat,' I said. 'Don't let them go without me.'

Tearlaich still hung back, apparently unable to drag his attention away from the garden. 'Those things, there,' he pointed. 'Are those trees?'

'They're supposed to be,' I confessed with a rueful glance at the row of baby conifers which I had planted early in the spring in the hope they would thrive and eventually provide natural shelter.

'They don't look as if they'll like to live,' observed Tearlaich without optimism.

'I doubt it very much myself,' I agreed, assessing the miniature branches which still showed faint traces of green tips but otherwise looked as if they had been pressed and scorched with a hot iron.

'Where did you get them?' asked Tearlaich.

'From that tinker. You know, the one they always call "Buggy Duck". He promised me last year he'd bring some next time he was round and this spring he turned up with these.'

'Were they like this when you got them?'

I nodded.

'I hope you didn't give him money for them?'

I admitted that I had paid Buggy Duck the price he had asked.

'Ach, I could have got you a few from the laird's place if I'd known you wanted them. He'd never miss that many.'

'I don't want illicit trees in my garden,' I said firmly.

Tearlaich looked at me and there were both pity and amazement in his expression. 'Why then did you ask Buggy Duck to bring you some?' he demanded. 'Like as not they came from the laird's place anyway but not so fresh as you'd have got them from me.' He threw the conifers a final disdainful glance as he turned away. 'I doubt they'll live the winter,' he informed me. 'They've been too dry.'

'I told Buggy Duck when he brought them they looked too dry to survive but he got quite indignant. He said they couldn't possibly have got too dry because he'd been sleeping with them inside his bedding for the last three months.'

Tearlaich and I exchanged amused glances. 'If a tinker's been sleeping with them for three months I doubt you'll have a lot of other things growing in your garden supposing you don't get any trees,' he comforted.

Even standing on the shore I could see the boat was grossly overloaded and when we came alongside in the dinghy I estimated there was hardly more than eighteen inches of freeboard. There were coy screams from some of the young girls aboard as Tearlaich jumped heavily on the gunwale causing the boat to rock spectacularly.

'She's fairly ready to sink with the weight of folks in her,' Erchy told him with a touch of irritation.

'Ach, it's calm enough,' retorted Tearlaich and squeezing himself between two of the girls sat grinning cheerfully with an arm round each of them.

It was a lustrous evening of velvet calm with remnants of the sunset still glowing behind the dark hill peaks and the unruffled sea reflecting the pale celadon of the sky save where the outlying islands cast sable shadows. Sea birds were everywhere, puffins, guillemots and razorbills, all bobbing and diving for late suppers while above them terns wheeled and dipped in flight.

Erchy assessed the number of heads aboard. 'Where's Johnny Mor?' he asked. 'He swore he was comin'.'

'I've seen no sign of him,' said Tearlaich. 'Ach, he was out on the hill today seein' to his sheep. Maybe he's fallen in a bog.'

'Well, if he has we're not waitin' till he gets out of it,' said Hector with a bland smile. He started the engine while Erchy attended to the mooring of the dinghy.

'Are we no' takin' the dinghy?' asked Hector as the rope was cast off.

'No damty fear,' replied Erchy. 'If nobody comes to meet us at Rhuna Miss Peckwitt can swim ashore an' get a hold of one of their dinghies.' I gave him an arch glance. I am a poor swimmer but the fact that I could keep afloat in the water at all astonished the Bruachites. The skirl of compassionate murmurings directed at me from the female passengers gave way to small shrieks and squeaks of excitement as the bow of the boat cut a sweeping arc through the water and turned towards Rhuna. The postman soon produced a mouth-organ and gradually coaxed most of the passengers into the singing of Gaelic and Scottish songs, the mixed choir of voices surging and ebbing over the water while the throbbing of the engine and the strains of the mouth-organ compounded into a makeshift orchestra.

'When you're on the sea,' Erchy had once confided to me, 'you either want to sing or you want to swear.' I stole a glance at him as he stood with one hand on the tiller, his head raised and his mouth wide open as he sang lustily. I watched the receding shore, the feeding birds and the evening settling over the water.

'Oh, look! A seal!' I cried as a sleek dark head bobbed out of the sea about fifty yards behind us. The rest of the company turned to give the seal a moment or two of its attention and then the singers, whose voices had only wavered at my interruption, were at full volume again. It was sometimes difficult for me to remember that sights which thrilled me were to the Bruachites so regular as to be commonplace; that they were as used to the presence of seals around their shores as I had once been to the presence of hawkers in town.

'There's another of them been following us for the past twenty minutes if you're that keen to see them,' shouted Tearlaich. 'It's the singing that brings them.'

'I sing nearly every time I go out in a boat,' I yelled back, 'but I've never managed to lure a seal to follow me yet.'

From the stern of the boat Erchy's voice came piercingly. 'That's because you sing in English. It's only the Gaelic that attracts them.'

For some time the two seals accompanied us, submerging and re-emerging at varying distances from the boat but always it seemed keeping us under observation with such timid yearning in their large dark eyes I was reminded of pictures of hungry waifs locked out from a feast.

As we approached the dark mass of Rhuna the island slowly yielded up its secrets. The bastion-like cliffs revealed themselves as being riven into steep sea-washed caverns and tiny shingle coves; shadowy hollows betrayed the entrances to secret caves; craggy pillars of rock were tenanted by uneasy shags, while on the tumbled boulders, still wet from the retreating tide, stood confident gulls watching us with half-hearted interest. Erchy steered the boat toward the mouth of a burn where two dinghies were moored by ropes to the shore. While we watched two men came out from one of the cottages and began to pull in both dinghies preparatory to rowing out to meet us.

'It's Roddy an' Calum that's comin',' announced Erchy. Hector stopped the engine. 'Aye, an' seein' tsey're bringin' two dinghies they must know we have a good load,' he observed.

'They're no' blind, are they?' Tearlaich told him.

If the boat had been overloaded the dinghies were even more so, there being barely three inches of freeboard on either of them. But no one worried. It was a calm evening and a short row. We clambered out on to the shingle without mishap.

'The cailleach has a strupach ready,' said Roddy, thus obliquely conveying to us that whoever we might wish to visit during the evening the real ceilidh was to be at his mother's house. She had staked her claim to our company.

'We'd best away an' get our hazels first,' Erchy told him. 'We'll take a strupach when we get back.'

'I'll take a look in at her,' Morag promised. 'But I couldn't swallow a mouthful till I've undone myself from the knot I was in aboard that boat. Indeed my legs was that stiff I thought I'd have to leave them behind.' She rubbed her knuckles into the small of her back.

'I want to go and see that apple tree,' I said firmly.

Rhuna boasted an apple tree which was reputed to have been grown from the pips of apples washed ashore when an American schooner foundered off the island during the Great War and on a previous visit, late in the autumn, I had discovered beneath the tree two rotting apples which I had taken home and planted. Despite lavish attention, however, the seeds had not germinated and, since I hoped to try again, I wanted to go and inspect the tree to satisfy myself it was still flourishing.

'I'll come along with you,' said Behag promptly. It transpired that most of the party had friends they wished to see or things they wished to do before gathering for a final strupach so it was agreed that Roddy was to tell his mother we would all return in about an hour's time for our ceilidh with her. The party therefore split up into various groups and went their different ways. Behag and I were joined by Tearlaich and by Roddy's brother, Calum, who, because he had spent much of his time at sea, was almost a stranger to Behag and to me. We ambled along slowly and Morag, who had nipped into the cottage to exchange polite greetings with the 'cailleach', soon caught up with us.

'You didn't tell me your sister Marie was home,' she accused Calum.

'Aye, she's home. She's gettin' married at the back end to some doctor or other so she's home for a rest first.'

'She'll need a rest first if she's goin' to marry a doctor,' remarked Tearlaich with an obscure smile.

'To a doctor,' echoed Morag. 'Do I know of him?'

'Indeed I don't know him myself,' returned Calum, 'except that he's from some hospital in Glasgow where she was once nursin'.'

'Aye, well, I've no doubt the girl will do well for herself,' said Morag in much the same tone as I might have said, 'She could do worse, I suppose.'

We followed Calum along an erratic track that skirted rags of crofts where tousled grass contested with drifts of heather its right to grow among the innumerable outcrops of stone. Calum stopped frequently to point out places of interest.

'It was just there my father dug up a barrel of salt butter when I was a boy,' he told us. 'An' it was still good.'

'An' how long would that have been there?' asked Morag.

'God knows,' replied Calum. 'Twenty-five years maybe. There was nobody livin' then who remembered it bein' put there.'

'That's most interesting,' I commented.

'I'd be more interested if you dug up a barrel of whisky,' countered Tearlaich wistfully.

'An' that was a fairy house, there,' said Calum at another juncture, indicating a smooth green mound covered with flat stones. 'An' this we're comin' to is what's always known as the "Red Burn".'

'Why red?' I asked.

'Because of all the blood that flowed in it.' His tone became grave. 'In days long ago, Miss Peckwitt, there was a wicked factor lived hereabouts an' once every year the crofters used to gather here to pay him their rents. Any man that couldn't pay was just murdered an' his body thrown into the burn. That's how it came to be known as the "Red Burn".' He looked at Morag. 'You'll surely have heard the story?'

'They say it was all true, right enough,' agreed Morag.

'It must have been,' asserted Calum. 'Why else would the cows refuse to drink from it, even to this day? No, nor walk through it, even.'

44

'Is that so?' asked Tearlaich with polite interest.

'It is so,' maintained Calum. 'I've seen a cow that's been tethered all day on the croft without water an' when she was loosed she made straight for the well on the moors sooner than go anywhere near that burn.'

'There must be the smell of murder in it yet,' declared Morag with apparent conviction.

'Aye, an' another thing,' continued Calum. 'Supposin' the cows are over this side of the island an' you need to drive them back to the crofts you can put half a dozen people an' dogs on to their tails but the beasts will never cross that burn. You'd have to walk a good mile out of your way an' beyond the loch before you'd get them home.'

We crossed the 'Red Burn' by the stepping stones and in doing so I noticed a promising-looking clump of watercress growing on one of its boggy banks.

'Look, watercress!' I pointed it out to Behag. I turned to Calum. 'Tell me,' I said, 'do the people of Rhuna believe like the Bruach people that watercress should be left for the fairies?'

'Aye, so they do.' He nodded back towards the burn. 'I seen a couple of them here the other night just, gatherin' great bunches of it.'

'Fairies?' I asked.

'Aye.'

'Did you see them yourself?' breathed Behag in an awestruck whisper.

'I did. I was out after a rabbit an' I came back this way pretty late an' there they were. I saw them as plain as I'm seein' you.'

'How did you know they were fairies?' I asked in a steady voice.

'Who else would be wearin' little green jackets an' red caps,' he retorted with a trace of asperity. Behag and I exchanged quick glances.

Our path led us towards a lichen-patterned heap of stones which had once enclosed a small patch of ground and I was delighted to see the apple tree not only growing vigorously but bearing an abundant crop of sizable though still unripe fruit. Tearlaich picked one but after tasting it he threw it nonchalantly in the direction of a late lingering hoodie crow which was picking at an ancient cowpat. Calum volunteered to bring me over a creelful of apples as soon as they were ripe if the Lord spared him.

'Now you've seen your tree is it not time we got away back to the house?' asked Morag.

'Ach, there's plenty time,' argued Calum. 'If the tea's cold the kettle will boil again.'

Morag was looking curiously at a ruined house nearby. 'Is that not the place the filmies burned?' she asked Calum.

'Aye, that's it.'

'They really burned down a house for making a film here?' I questioned.

'They did, but it was a ruin before they burned it mostly. They got my Uncle Alistair an' my cousin John to build up the front of it an' put a bitty thatch on so that it looked all right to the cameras but it was no more than a ruin for all that.'

'Was it not your Uncle Alistair that let them have the house to burn?' pursued Morag.

'Aye, it was him.'

'I heard he got good money for it,' Tearlaich observed.

'I believe he did,' admitted Calum. 'Ach, an' why not?' he continued. 'Those filmies were right daft with their money.'

'That's what I was after hearin' myself,' said Morag enviously.

Calum chuckled. 'Right enough, at first Alistair was makin' out his own father was born in that ruin an' so the old place meant a lot to him still.'

46

'Was his father born there?' I asked.

'He was not. Alistair just wanted to push up the price he could put on it but the filmies were that convinced they started askin' around for men to build them just enough of a place to fool the cameras. Alistair got so scared they'd do it he went an' offered the ruin to the filmies for fifty pounds so long as he and his son got the job of building it up for them. I believe he had to have a good drink on him before he could pluck up courage to ask such a high price but the filmies jumped at it. When he got home he was as sick as a dog for not havin' asked double.'

'Were you home yourself the time the filmies were here?' asked Behag.

'I was. Indeed I was in the film myself,' Calum replied.

'You were?' exclaimed Behag admiringly.

'Aye. I played one of these extras, they call them. We all did at one time or another. They paid us well for it too. I tell you they was daft with their money. In the evenin' when we went to draw what was owin' to us they paid everybody that was in sight whether they'd been workin' for them or not. Hamish Beag came ashore in his boat one time, just, after bein' out fishin' but when he passed the place where the man was payin' out the money he was called over an' handed the same pay as the rest of us. I've never seen a man look as surprised as Hamish looked then, I can tell you.'

'Why would they do that?' asked Morag, puzzled.

'Ach, they didn't seem as if they could tell one from another of us no more than I can tell one black man from another.' He chuckled again reminiscently. 'We got a good laugh out of those filmies an' all.'

'An' good money,' Morag reminded him again. 'There was a few in Bruach would have come over to work for the filmies if they'd got the chance. Why, they tell me even old Kenny Mor, him that was so religious he wouldn't so much as boil a kettle on the Sabbath an' yet he was earnin' money for himself makin' tea for them.'

'He was so,' agreed Calum. 'An' Kenny fairly enjoyed himself doin' it until the missionary came over one Sunday an' preached that films was sinful an' anybody that worked for them would go straight to hell.'

'An' did anybody take any notice?' asked Morag.

'Only Kenny Mor,' rejoined Calum. 'He gave up the job an' the money for fear of goin' to hell.'

'Ach, the missionary was just jealous,' summed up Tearlaich. 'I doubt he wanted to make the tea for them himself.'

'Where are you takin' us to now?' demanded Morag as Calum led us on through a narrow strath of swampy ground so liberally tasselled with bog-cotton it looked as if an eiderdown had burst over it.

'Just a wee way yet,' he told her.

We followed, pushing our way through a tough little corrie black with waist-high dead heather; over wide slabs of weathered rock and then along a poachy path, rumpled with hoof prints and leading into a miniature birchwood which in turn petered out as it met the rocks and shingle of the shore.

'Who can that be?' asked Morag, stopping in her tracks. A man and a woman were coming away from the beach, the woman bent under a burden of driftwood that was roped to her shoulders while the man carried only a few short lengths of wood under his left arm. In his right hand he held a slim pole which he was using as a walking stick.

'That's Dolina an' Mata,' Calum told her.

Although it was impossible for our paths not to bring us face to face, Morag immediately began to shout greetings in strident Gaelic which diminished in volume as the distance between us decreased. By the time we did meet all the initial pleasantries were disposed of and they were ready to converse in English. Dolina, whose tall, utility-built body seemed to be packed full of bones, was obviously delighted to see us. With strong hands and in no way constrained by the load she carried she pulled first Morag, then Behag, then myself into a warm embrace which was intense enough to make me gasp, and in the brisk whisper that was her normal speaking voice she begged us to be sure to take a strupach with her before leaving the island. Here, however, Calum stepped in, jealously guarding his mother's privilege, and advised her of the proposed ceilidh, whereupon Dolina declared that nothing save a cow calving or the end of the world would keep her from joining the company. 'Is that not so, Mata?' she addressed her husband.

In contrast with Dolina, Mata looked as if he had been expertly filleted; his handshake was flabby and his bulging grey eyes looked about as ardent as two water blisters on the point of bursting, but he managed by a swift raising and lowering of his eyebrows to convey that he too would be coming to the ceilidh.

'We'd best not keep you back,' said Morag after a while and having been thus politely dismissed Dolina and Mata went on their way.

'I wish to goodness he'd carry her load for her,' I said as soon as they were out of earshot.

'Indeed Dolina wouldn't allow it,' stated Morag.

'He'd never have married her if he thought she'd let him,' added Tearlaich.

I murmured something about his being a shirker.

'But poor Mata doesn't enjoy good health,' Morag excused him.

'Damty sure he doesn't,' Tearlaich rejoined. 'That man only enjoys himself when he's sick.'

'Oh, whisht, now,' chided Morag, chuckling in spite of herself. 'All the same,' she added after a pause, 'there's somethin' about that man I canna help mislikin'.'

'I mislike him myself,' Tearlaich agreed and added, almost confidentially, 'I'll tell you, he's a disgustin' bugger that one.'

'I haven't seen him do anything positive enough to be disgusting,' I told him. 'Except, of course, leaving Dolina to do all the heavy work and he's not the only man around here who's guilty of that.'

'It's the way it's always been since I remember,' interpolated Morag. 'An' right enough that's the way many of the women want it to be.'

'I wasn't thinking of him being disgusting like that,' Tearlaich denied. 'But I was on the bus with him once and he started shouting he wanted to pee. He made the driver stop and he got out but instead of going some place where he wouldn't be seen he just stood and peed beside the bus like a tracehorse. Honest to God! And there was tourists aboard too. I didn't know where to look I was that ashamed of him.'

'That was ignorant of him,' Morag agreed. 'Poor Dolina would have died had she seen him.'

'I can't help feeling sorry for Dolina,' I said.

'I feel sorry for her myself,' concurred Tearlaich, 'but all the same I was near laughing when I saw her hugging you three as if you were children.'

'An' isn't it because she has no children of her own that makes her want to hug people,' Morag reproved him. 'A woman like Dolina ought by nature to have children at her skirts.'

'Aye, right enough, but not you three grown women.' From his expression I guessed he had been about to say 'old women' and had only just caught himself in time. 'It's not

Highland,' he added, much as an Englishman would have said 'It's not done'.

'Mata didn't marry Dolina to give her children,' asserted Calum. 'The reason he married her was to quiet his sister.'

'That's not what I heard then,' Morag rebutted his statement indignantly. 'Surely his sister was that jealous of Mata takin' a wife if it hadn't been for Dolina's good nature they would have quarrelled every day of the week – except the Sabbath,' she added.

'She was jealous all right,' confirmed Calum. 'But all the same it was her that made him take Dolina.'

'Why did she insist on his marrying?' I asked.

'Because she'd never in her life laid in a bed by herself till her mother died. She had another sister an' they slept together until that sister died. Then she moved into her mother's bed an' when she died there was no one to share her bed so she girned at Mata to find another woman to lie beside her.'

'But shouldn't she have got married herself or at least found someone to share her bed?' I asked. I could not seriously believe that a man would get married simply to provide a sleeping partner for his sister.

'Aye, but you see she claimed it was her home as much as Mata's, which is right enough seein' she was born there. Mata got the croft but the house belongs to those born in it, so she said. Anyway Mata's such a poor thing he just took a quick look around an' there was Dolina who'd have thrown herself into a bog for any man. It was easy as that an' it kept his sister quiet.'

'An' has Dolina never shared her man's bed?' expostulated Morag.

'Never,' averred Calum. 'Mata told me so himself.'

'He must have an orra chomais on him,' quipped Tearlaich, and we all laughed.

'He's a detestable fellow,' I commented.

'But Dolina loves him like the sun,' Morag reminded me simply.

'Aye an' that's why she's glad to do the heavy carryin' to save Mata doin' it,' said Calum. 'Seein' she's not allowed to do the little things for him that a wife likes to do for her man. The sister does the cookin' and washin' his clothes an' puttin' out his slippers in an evenin'. Dolina just washes the dishes an' does most of the work of the croft.'

'An' never a word of complaint on her lips, I doubt,' added Morag.

'St Dolina of Rhuna,' I murmured.

'Aye, if you believe in saints she must be one,' agreed Calum.

'Now we're here why have you brought us here?' Morag stood looking about her curiously.

'I have a thing to show you that I found down on the shore,' replied Calum. 'Wait you now till I get it.'

He made towards a pile of boulders and crouching he appeared to be extricating something from a deep crevice. Having retrieved it he came back to us. 'See this!' he said, holding up a small canister with a screw top.

We had all been expecting Calum to produce some really unusual or valuable find and our disappointment at seeing such an apparently uninteresting object was plain.

'What is it?' asked Tearlaich.

'It's a body!' announced Calum dramatically.

'A body?' Behag's question came out in an incredulous squeak.

'Aye, see this now. Can you read it?' Calum held the canister nearer towards me as I backed away. 'That says somethin' about a crematorium, does it not? That's where they cremate bodies.'

Tearlaich took the canister and examined it. 'Aye, you're right,' he said. 'Did you open it yet?'

'I did,' Calum admitted. 'But open it yourself an' take a look at it.'

Tearlaich did as Calum suggested and tilted the canister so as to see inside it. 'It's full of stuff like that guano we had one year for the potatoes.' He handed the canister back to Calum who emptied out a little of its contents on to the palm of his hand.

'Are you sure it's a body?' asked Behag doubtfully.

'Sure it is,' declared Calum. He licked his forefinger and dipped it into the powder. 'Here,' he held his finger towards her. 'Taste it if you like,' he invited without the ghost of a smile.

Behag turned away and I was not sure whether she was giggling or vomiting.

'What are you goin' to do with it?' asked Morag.

'Damned if I know,' said Calum.

'Ach, give it to Miss Peckwitt for her garden,' Tearlaich proposed. 'It'll make good fertiliser.'

Calum screwed back the top and was about to hand me the canister but I recoiled away from it. 'D'you not want it?' he asked in surprise.

'I do not,' I said firmly. 'I'd never sleep at night if I thought someone's body was spread out among the flowers in my garden. I think you should throw it back in the sea,' I advised.

'It'll only get washed ashore again,' said Calum, shaking the canister with absent-minded vigour. 'Maybe you're right, though,' he continued after a few moments. 'I might just as well throw it back seein' the tide's goin' out anyway. It'll maybe take it to someone else's beach.' He went down to the tide's edge and hurled the canister away into the sea.

'I don't know why you didn't take it for your garden,' Tearlaich rebuked me. 'Bone meal's one of the best manures you can get.' I tried to quell him with a look.

Calum rejoined us. 'I know a woman once whose husband was very fond of growin' roses,' he told us. 'When he died she had him cremated an' his ashes put on his favourite rose bushes.'

'Never!' Morag's voice was a disapproving groan. 'It's true,' he asseverated. 'She used to go out an' talk to them every night. Said it was like havin' her husband there out in the garden, an' when she used to prune them she used to pretend she was cuttin' his toenails for him like she always used to when he was alive.'

'She was mad, surely,' said Morag.

Calum raised his eyebrows in perfunctory agreement.

'Talking of such things brings to mind a story my commanding officer used to tell,' recalled Tearlaich. 'Seemingly at one time in India it used to be against the law for the natives to make their own salt. They were supposed to buy it from the government but some of the natives used to know where they could get earth that was full of salt and they'd wash it and then dry it in the sun till there was only salt left. If they were caught doing it they were up before the judge and one day the pollis got one old woman actually with a bag of this illegal salt in her possession, or so they claimed. Anyway, up she came before the court and the judge asked her what was in her bag but the old woman wouldn't say a word or plead one way or the other. The judge was just tellin' her he was goin' to fine her one rupee for disobeying the law when he suddenly thinks he'd best make sure it really was salt in the bag so he calls for a spoon and dips it in the bag and just as he's puttin' it into his mouth the old woman speaks for the first time. "This is a wicked court," she shouts, "not only do they fine me one rupee but they also eat the ashes of my dead husband."'

'Oh God,' murmured Behag with a feeble attempt at a giggle. Tearlaich gave her an arch look. 'It's true,' he insisted.

'True or not,' interrupted Morag firmly, 'that's enough of your stories for tonight. We'd best get back to the cailleach or she'll be thinkin' we're in a bog.'

Although it was after midnight there was only a little fuzzing of the light while among the dark hill peaks the afterglow still threaded itself like a bright scarf. It was impossible to know if the rosy rock pools were reflecting the sunset or the dawn. I recalled Masefield's lines:

> 'By an intense glow the evening falls,
> Bringing not darkness but a deeper light.'

and thought how perfectly they described the evening. Over the moors snipe drummed and closer at hand there were still sporadic trickles of birdsong.

'I wonder if Erchy and Hector are back with their hazels yet,' I mused.

'Their hazels?' echoed Tearlaich with some bewilderment.

'Yes. That's what they went for, isn't it?'

'Surely,' agreed Tearlaich, a little too eagerly. He and Calum exchanged cryptic glances. Morag avoided looking at me. I pinned my enquiring glance on Behag.

'You surely didn't think they came here just for the hazels?' she asked gently.

'But that's what they told me they were coming for,' I argued. 'That and to have a ceilidh at the same time.'

There was compassion and amusement in the four pairs of eyes that regarded me.

'Likely they will get their hazels seein' they'll soon be needin' them for the creels,' Behag admitted.

'Aye, an' everyone likes a wee bit of a ceilidh,' interposed Morag.

'But that's not what they came for?' I challenged, beginning to smile.

'Did you no' see the net under the seats of the boat?' asked Behag with an answering smile.

'How could she not see it when her own two feets was planted on it?' declared Morag.

I had indeed observed a net under the seats but I knew little about the type of net needed for the catching of different fish and in my ignorance I had thought it was an old herring net my feet rested on.

'It's a bit risky over there, isn't it?' I said. 'Didn't Erchy say the police are pretty keen to catch the poachers in that river?'

'Aye, they're keen,' agreed Tearlaich fervently. 'They'll even go there on their nights off and hide themselves in the hope of catching a poacher's boat. Folks say that the sergeant gets a good salmon from the laird every time he catches a poacher.'

'And yet Erchy and Hector aren't afraid of getting caught?'

'They won't get caught,' asserted Morag confidently.

I gave her a sidelong glance but she only smiled.

'Erchy has a sign,' explained Tearlaich. 'He's arranged with Jimmy's wife that lives in one of the houses near the shore that if there's a pair of long underpants on the clothes-line then the pollis are hidin' somewhere about an' he mustn't go near. If the clothes-line is empty he's safe.'

'An' Erchy will not get caught so long as Jimmy has a spare pair of underpants his wife can hang on the line,' observed Morag.

'Ach, if she's no spare underpants she'll just hang Jimmy on the clothes-line,' said Tearlaich, and added after a moment's thought: 'Right enough, I believe she'd do that for Erchy.'

56

The Men who Played with the Fairies

The window of Calum's mother's cottage was a token of light in the after-midnight dusk, and through the open door, interwoven with the murmur of voices, swooned the vague strains of the postie's mouth-organ. Calum left us abruptly and disappeared round the back of the house and Morag and Behag, panting for tea, hurried inside. As they entered, Erchy emerged carrying a cup of tea in one hand and the remains of a thick wad of dumpling in the other. He sat himself down on an upturned tub beneath the window.

'Any luck?' enquired Tearlaich.

One side of Erchy's face bulged as he cached a large bite of dumpling in order to reply.

'Plenty of luck,' he said thickly. His eyes glistened with excitement. 'You should have been there I'm tellin' you.'

'How could I be when I was keepin' the women out of the way?' returned Tearlaich reasonably.

'Aye, but you'd best have come with us,' reiterated Erchy.

'Aye?' Tearlaich's voice was sharp with interest.

Erchy nodded emphatically. 'There was one of the monsters went clean through the net. The biggest salmon I've seen yet,' he added impressively. He took a gulp of tea. 'We got a good laugh out of it all, I can tell you.'

'You got a good laugh out of losin' a big salmon an' gettin' a hole in your net? It's a queer comic you are, then,' Tearlaich commented.

'Not out of that just but out of Hector,' Erchy elucidated. 'He was that mad when we lost the big fellow he jumped into the river himself an' tried to stop the rest gettin' through. There was about a dozen fish in the net then an' Hector was so feared they'd get away he threw his arms round the biggest one an' held on to it. He'd barely caught hold of it when he got his foot caught in the net an' he sat down on his bottom in the river still clutchin' this huge fish an' it jumpin' an' twistin' like a serpent.' Erchy slopped tea as he used his arms to illustrate Hector's predicament. ' "Hit it! Hit it! Erchy!" he shouts at me. Well I was seein' if I could close the net first but I managed to grab hold of a stick at the same time. "Hit it, you fool!" yells Hector, gettin' awful wild with me because he thought I wasn't helpin' him. "How can I hit it when it's first your head an' then the salmon's where the stick would land?" says I. It was one of them big male salmon with the huge jaw an' that great hook they have on it.' Erchy put down both cup and dumpling on the window-sill and spread his arms to indicate the size of the salmon. 'My God! there was some power in it too. The beast kept leapin' up an' Hector kept pullin' it down hand over hand like a man climbin' a rope. "Get your jersey over it!" I shouted to him, so he pulls up his jersey an' wraps the salmon in it while I see to the net. I went to help him then but God! if only you'd seen him gettin' to the shore with the fish still jumpin' up an' down inside his jersey an' him fightin' it an' swearin' an' stumblin' over the rocks you would have laughed fit to cry.' Erchy shook his head slowly. 'You should have been there.'

'Did he manage to get his salmon ashore?' I asked.

'Aye, he did. An' most of the rest. We were lucky. We got eight altogether,' he replied with deep satisfaction. 'That's a good night's work for any two men.'

'And you holed your net,' Tearlaich reminded him. 'Was it in much of a state?'

'Not as much of a state as was Hector's jersey,' responded Erchy. 'That's why I came out here. I'm best out of the way for when Behag catches sight of it. She only finished knittin' it for him last week just.'

I left the two men talking and went into the cottage where already round about twenty people were compressed into the small room. It was obvious that some more sophisticated hand had been at work on the old croft kitchen; the floor was covered with tile-patterned linoleum; the wooden walls and the dresser were a glossy apple green; the dignified wall clock looked a little surprised to find its frame painted in bright yellow and indeed the whole room though it looked fresh and cheerful struck me as having the faintly startled air of a tramp who has been compelled to wear a smart new suit.

Calum's mother greeted me with a lengthy handshake and the rest, all of whom I knew by sight, acknowledged me with grins or nods or murmurs of welcome according to their degree of shyness. Morag tried to make room for me to sit beside her on the crowded bench but I selected a more comfortable seat on the floor where, within minutes, I was joined by Behag who brought me a cup of tea.

'I don't see anyone here who could be Calum's sister Marie,' I whispered. Behag looked blank. 'You know, the one who's going to marry a doctor.'

'Oh!' Behag glanced round. 'I believe she's just away for a pail of water,' she told me. 'They're needin' more, likely, seein' there's been a few fillin's of the kettle already an' I daresay there'll be more before the night's over.'

There came from outside the clink of pails followed by some male chaffing to which everyone strained to listen, then a laughing retort in a female voice that sounded as melodious as a harp. A tall, strongly built woman, gum-booted and wearing a sad old skirt and an overtight jersey, entered the room followed by Erchy gallantly carrying two slopping pails of water. The woman cleared a small table beside the door for Erchy to put down the pails and turned to smile a confident greeting. Although Calum's mother was in her eighties and Calum himself was nudging fifty I had foolishly been expecting the prospective bride to be a younger woman, forgetting that in Bruach a spinster is referred to as a girl be she seventeen or seventy. Marie, I estimated after a brief appraisal, was probably in her forties but she was still a strikingly handsome woman. Her skin was smooth and white as a dawn-picked mushroom; her bee-tawny eyes were wide and lively; her abundant russet-coloured hair swathed her head in soft waves until it was caught by a crocheted wool snood. She came forward and shaking my hand made me welcome in so attractive a voice it would have made scurrility sound like a serenade.

'We're awful quiet, are we not?' she observed after a few moments. 'Hector, now! What about you givin' us a song?'

Hector looked pleased but shook his head. 'I've swallowed tsat much of tse river tonight I'd only gargle,' he replied. 'What about a song from you yourself, Marie?'

'Oh, I can't sing,' denied Marie firmly, and to my surprise there was not even a polite contradiction. She turned to Morag. 'Morag here's good at the singin'. What about you? Give us a song now an' the rest will join in.'

Whether or not Morag would have complied I do not know for just at that moment a tall, fair-haired man pushed his way through the men clustered around the doorway. He was wearing a cap and what was undoubtedly his best raincoat. In his hand was a folded sack tied with string which he carried like a shopping bag. Immediately he appeared there were screams of expectant laughter and everyone settled down to enjoy themselves. Putting his sack on the table the man extracted from it a crescent of wire attached to a length of thin rope. He beckoned one of the young girls to sit down beside him and since everyone knew what was about to happen the girl quickly complied. Pretending the wire and the piece of rope were his stethoscope he set about examining the girl's chest, back and head and while the girl giggled the man listened and groaned, hunted in his bag for more instruments, mimed swabbing and surgery, stitching and bandaging and with silent gesticulation kept his hilarious audience informed of what the various ailments were and how he proposed to treat them. Though, like the rest, this was by no means the first time I had witnessed his act, I laughed and applauded along with them. But my enjoyment was feigned. Undoubtedly the mime was good and the performer delighted by our appreciation but I would have enjoyed it more had I not known that the actor was not only deaf and dumb but also mentally retarded; that mime was indeed his sole means of communication. Known as 'the Dummy', he was a gentle soul, glum when he observed others to be glum; happy when he saw them happy; and having once discovered that some of his attempts to communicate brought smiles to people's faces he had exaggerated his mime until their smiles had erupted into laughter. It was all he asked. He had made people happy and consequently he insisted on performing at every ceilidh on the island. Since the doctor-and-patient mime made people laugh he saw no reason to change it though it had continued for the ten years since the doctor had last visited the island.

'Not that one grows tired of it,' confided one of 'the Dummy's' neighbours. 'But you sometimes wish somebody more interesting than a doctor would visit the island to give the poor man something else to imitate.'

'What about the filmies?' I asked.

'Ah, he was only a poor thing then,' she explained. 'He hadn't discovered his gift.'

When 'the Dummy's' performance was over Erchy spoke up. 'Marie's goin' to give us the sword dance,' he announced, and treated the company to a heavy wink. He put his arm around Marie's waist and tickled her vigorously. She pushed him away.

'Indeed I will do nothing of the kind,' she declined but the pleading that she should dance for us became so clamorous – 'maybe for the last time, seein' you're to get yourself married' – that she was finally persuaded. We squeezed ourselves even more tightly back against the wall so as to make sufficient space in the centre of the room. The shuffling revealed the presence of a child of about four years who had previously been hidden by his mother's skirts but who now peeped out timidly from among them like a chick peeping from among the feathers of the mother hen. It also revealed that behind the legs of the people seated on the bench lay a sheepdog watching the proceedings with eyes that in the lamplight glowed large and round as gold medals. There was some discussion as to what could be used for swords but Erchy was soon flourishing four brass rods taken from the linoleum stair runner and handing them to Marie to arrange into a cross on the floor. The postman retrieved his mouth-organ from the lad who had been blowing into it unskilfully and began to play. Marie kicked off her gumboots and barefooted commenced the intricate dance in and out of the 'swords', slowly at first but as the postman increased the tempo of the music so did her pace quicken until her feet appeared to be fluttering above the floor rather than touching it. It was an impressive performance and young and old shrieked and stamped their admiration until Marie, declaring herself to be utterly out of breath, abruptly ceased dancing to a chorus of disappointed 'Ahs'.

'I could do with watchin' that all over again,' said Erchy. 'Oh, help!' gasped Marie and snatching off her snood shook her head so that her hair cascaded soft and springy as a child's around her shoulders. I noticed Tearlaich staring at her with wide-eyed adulation.

'That's made me as dry as a stick!' she exclaimed and picking up the teapot she poured herself a cup of tea.

'I'll be takin' anotser myself,' said Hector, and by handing her his empty cup started a chain reaction so that there was suddenly a flurry of cups all being passed for refilling. It appeared that the dancing had induced a great thirst among the onlookers also. The room quietened as they sipped.

Calum spoke. 'I was after tellin' Miss Peckwitt I'd seen the fairies gatherin' the biolaire by the Red Burn the other evenin',' he informed the company in general. 'I doubt she wasn't believin' me,' he added dispassionately.

Calum's uncle, a seared old man with a raised furrow of white hair that ran like a partition across his otherwise close-cropped head, was slumped in a wooden chair beside the fire. At Calum's remark he sat up and shot me a glance from sharp black eyes that were set deep in a face as brown and rutted as a peach stone. He drew his pipe from his mouth and fondled it in a calloused hand. 'Ach, but she's from the town, is she not?' he excused me gently. 'There's no use speakin' to some about the wee folk. No use at all.' He shook his head sadly. 'But there's plenty round these parts that's seen them an' there's some that's been the better of it an' some that has not.'

I looked at him steadily but his eyes were fixed on the bowl of his pipe.

63

'Like the men who played with the fairies,' interposed Calum's mother in a low voice.

'Just that,' agreed the old man with a nod.

'I've heard of them before but just who were they?' I interposed.

'Wasn't one of them my own father's cousin's child,' he replied.

'You should have taken Miss Peckwitt to see the men who played with the fairies,' Calum's mother turned to Hector. 'It's not so long since they passed on. No more than three years I doubt.'

'Five,' corrected Calum.

'Well, five,' his mother allowed. 'But Miss Peckwitt's been in Bruach for more years than that, surely?'

'I have indeed,' I replied. 'But whenever I've heard them spoken of I always assumed they'd been dead for some time. Was it really only five years ago that they died?'

'No more than that,' confirmed Calum's uncle, shifting his gaze to the coloured plates on the dresser.

I was intrigued. The 'men who played with the fairies' had been mentioned more than once at the Bruach ceilidhs but I had always assumed them to be as remote as legend.

'These two men,' I pressed. 'I understood they were twins?'

'No, they were not then. Didn't I say one of them was my own father's cousin's child.'

'And who was the other one, then?'

'Yes, who was he?' The question came from the postie.

It became obvious that some of the younger Bruachites were not completely familiar with the story of the two men and their adventures and after one or two questions Calum's mother said: 'You'd best tell them the way of it as you know it yourself, for it's right that the truth should be known about these things.'

Obediently, putting his pipe on the hob, Calum's uncle settled himself for the story. 'I mind seein' the boys just before it happened,' he told us. 'My father took me with him over to the island where they lived to try would he find a good spot for gatherin' the whelks. Seein' his cousin was there we left the boat an' went up to have a wee crack with him. The both boys was there then: a few years younger than myself they were but I mind they were fine healthy lookin' lads though wee rascals I believe, the pair of them, and always playin' tricks on folks as though it was Hallowe'en all the year round. Robbie, that was my father's cousin's child, an' Euan, that was the son of Hamish the Seanachaidh, was about the same age within a month or two an' when they weren't needed to help on their parents' crofts they'd go off fishin' together or seekin' gulls' eggs or maybe settin' a snare or two for the rabbits.' The old man paused and standing up helped himself to a spoonful of baking soda from the tin on the mantleshelf. 'The next time I went with my father to the island,' he resumed as he sat down again, 'I was maybe in my fifteenth year an' like we did before we went to have a crack with my father's cousin. We didn't see either of the boys an' so my father asked after them, sayin' he hoped they were well. That's how we came to know the story.'

His body tautened; he gave a loud belch and relaxed again. I slid a surreptitious glance around the room and saw that except for Marie, who appeared to be asleep with her head resting against the wall, and her mother, who was gazing into her lap, everyone's attention was concentrated on the old man willing him, it seemed, to go on with his tale.

'Aye,' he said unhurriedly, leaning back and tucking his thumbs into the armholes of his waistcoat. 'We had the story of it there on the spot where it all came to pass.'

'What was it that happened?' I could not be sure who had spoken but the voice sounded young and impatient.

'What happened,' went on Calum's uncle, 'was that they went together off fishin' one day just the same as they'd gone before, but when the evenin' was darkenin' there came no word of either of them. They were about nine years old at the time an' good at playin' tricks as I've said before, an' nobody worried a great deal at first, thinkin' the boys was well able to look after themselves, but when it came to midnight an' past an' there was still no word of them the men set out to look for them. They went to all the places they knew the boys liked to go an' they shouted but never a whisper came back to them. The next day every able bodied man an' woman an' child in the place went lookin' for them over the moors, up an' down the cliffs an' along the shore thinkin' they might have fallen into the sea. But no. They looked till there was no place they could look and still there was no trace of Robbie an' Euan. On the fourth day they gave them up for lost when suddenly that same evenin' they see the two boys comin' down the hill towards the houses. At first folks thought it was ghosts they were seein', for the boys were walkin' that steady an' close to each other like they'd never done before; holdin' hands like little girls. "It's never them!" people said to one another but it was them right enough though there was such a change in them people looked at them like strangers. Their faces were white as if they'd been shut in the dark for a while an' the merry eyes of them had got grey an' dull like empty pails. They didn't look at their parents when they rushed to meet them but only stared in front of them without speakin' a word. It was just like they were blind an' yet they knew where they were goin', for they both made for Euan's house an' there they got into bed together as if they'd been sharin' a bed since they were wee. They slept without food or wakin' for near three more days an' their parents, thinkin' the boys would come to their senses after a good sleep, left them alone. But they never did. When they woke they still stared at their folks as if they were strangers an' they never spoke save in whispers to each other. They never smiled either an' when they moved they stayed that close to each other Robbie's father said it was like as if you were seein' one man with three legs walkin' about. He took it badly did Robbie's father but try as he would there was no doin' any good with either of the boys any more. He told us it was like lookin' at one man carryin' a mirror they copied each other so much.'

'Did they never say what happened to them during those four days?' asked the young Bruach schoolteacher.

'Never a word. No, they were useless. They wouldn't work on the crofts any more an' no one dared to try to force them. They knew then, d'you see, that the boys had played with the fairies an' until the wee folk lifted the spell they'd put on them they'd have to allow the boys to do as they pleased.'

'What did they do with themselves, then?' Behag enquired softly.

'Ach they just roamed the moors, gatherin' all sorts of plants an' flowers or they wandered along the shore collecting coloured pebbles an' pieces of wood an' things they showed no interest in before.' The old man belched again and picked up his pipe. 'An' that's the way they were for many a long year,' he told us.

'Did you ever see them again?' I asked.

'I saw them once more,' replied the old man. 'An' I'm tellin' you I was that taken back I didn't know what to say. They was middle-aged by then an' they'd grown so alike you'd have sworn it was a pair of twins they were.' He looked at me. 'That's how you would be hearin' they were twins,' he explained. 'I didn't remember there bein' any likeness between them when they were younger but now I couldn't tell one from the other. Where one had red hair the other was black but now they were both white as old fleece.'

'Did they still hold hands and move together?' asked the schoolteacher.

'Indeed they did,' replied the old man. 'Still fittin' their steps to each other's like soldiers on parade an' with such a strange look on them I didn't feel I wanted to stay near them.'

'I suppose they didn't recognise you,' someone said.

'It seemed like they didn't know anyone or want to know anyone. Euan's parents had died but he didn't seem to notice. His sister stayed lookin' after them though even she saw little enough of them.'

'Did Robbie never return to his own home?' Again it was I who put the question.

'Never. Not from the day the two boys came back an' got into bed together. It was as if Robbie had forgotten he'd ever had a home.'

'An' did they never go off again?' I could not tell whether Morag was making a statement or asking a question.

'No, they never did. But as soon as they were old enough they built themselves a shed at the back of the house an' that's where they spent most of their time.'

'What did they do in there?'

'Indeed for a long time no one knew what they did but seemingly the sister found out they'd taken to carving wood. Wee boats like toys with oars an' sails an' wee chairs an' tables no bigger than if they were for a doll's house. Not that they let people see them if they could help it. They worked on their own an' they kept the shed locked but the sister managed to get a peep in every now an' then an' tell of what she saw. An' that went on for years.'

'They must have made a good few things in that time, then,' someone observed. 'What did they do with them all?'

'What indeed?' replied Calum's uncle. 'No one knows except that once Robbie's sister was seekin' driftwood on the shore an' she came across one of their wee boats wedged among some rocks. It was smashed to pieces but all the same she took it home an' put it beside their shed. She said when they found it they were so upset she wished she'd left it where it was.'

'What happened eventually,' I prompted.

'They died,' said the old man. 'An' they was as queer about their dyin' as their livin'. It was like this, y'see. Euan's sister was after havin' these fly peeps from time to time into their shed an' she saw they were buildin' a far bigger boat than she'd seen before. It was small enough still but carved an' decorated so much she wondered how hands could be gentle enough to do it. They were busy at it for a year or more an' then one day they seemed to be so much happier, more like they should be, so while they were out she went for another peep an' saw the boat was finished. She wondered what would happen an' that night she heard them go off after dark as they sometimes did an' it was near daylight when she heard the house door close. In the mornin' she heard moans comin' from the bedroom an' when she went in she found Euan lying alone in the bed. He looked straight at her an' spoke her name for the first time in years, an' asked her for a drink of water. She took it to him an' he drank it an' seemed as though he would sleep again, but when she went back a whiley later he was dead, just.'

Ever since he had taken his pipe from the hob the old man had been fondling it but now he filled it and picking a blazing peat from the fire puffed it alight. Having sharpened our eagerness by the deliberate pause he resumed: 'An' where was Robbie, you'll be wantin' to know. Robbie was back in his own home an' his own bed as if he'd suddenly remembered it was his. His parents were old then an' they didn't know what to say but he was that hot an' lay tossin' an' turnin' an' bletherin' away like the wild geese passin' over, though they couldn't make out a word of what he was sayin', they told the nurse to come. She said he had pneumonia an' she tried to get hold of a doctor but before he could get over Robbie was dead too. They buried them together an' I went with my father to the funeral.'

'What happened about the boat they'd been buildin'?' asked Behag.

'Now that's the strange way of it,' replied Calum's uncle. 'When the sister got hold of the key of the shed an' opened it after the funeral the boat had gone. All that was left of their toys at all was the little wrecked boat she'd found and brought back to give them. Just that in a corner of the shed an' near covered with sawdust.'

'Surely someone must have found the boat?' I said.

'No one ever did.' The old man's voice was firm. 'An' from what the sister was sayin' it was a great shame indeed, because it was beautiful just an' somethin' a body would like to keep in memory.'

'I wonder what happened to it,' mused Behag. But no one suggested an answer.

The postie blew suddenly on his mouth-organ a long chord that could almost have been a raspberry.

Calum's uncle got up stiffly, stretched himself and went to stand at the open door. 'The light is awakenin',' he proclaimed, coming back to resume his seat.

Erchy, who appeared to have been dozing through much of the old man's tale, pulled himself up from the floor.

'One more song an' then we must be away,' he declared. 'Come on, everybody.' The postman began to play 'My ain Folk' and we belted it out with sad enthusiasm before we trouped down to the shore in time to a lilting version of 'Mairi's Wedding'. We said our goodbyes and thank yous for a 'grand ceilidh' and were rowed out to the boat which was already loaded with its additional cargo of hazels and illicit salmon. The night was quiet except for a few muted gull cries and the water was still, though patterned as if it was covered with wire netting.

'Where's that bundle of cordite you found on the shore?' Marie's voice came clearly and we saw her run to the byre and return with a bundle which she hastily distributed among the crowd gathered to see us off. They lit the bundles and waved flaring farewells. To the strains of 'Will ye no come back again' echoing from the shore the boat chugged Bruachwards through a sea that was the colour of smoked glass. It was cold on the water and I was glad that lack of space necessitated our huddling together. Tearlaich's breadth was on one side of me and Behag's comfortable rotundity on the other. Erchy, who was again at the tiller, crouched behind us.

'I'm thinkin' that Marie's a big woman to be as light on her feet as she was,' observed Behag thoughtfully.

'Mmm,' I agreed. 'They often are, these big women. She's good-looking though, isn't she?' I went on. 'And her voice was beautiful and so was her hair...'

'Aye, her hair,' interrupted Tearlaich eagerly. 'Now Marie's hair's the sort of hair I'd want a woman of mine to have. An' did you see when she snatched off that net she had on the way it all fell as soon as it was loosed?'

'I saw,' I told him. 'And I noticed how overcome with admiration you were.'

71

'Indeed that's true,' he agreed fervently. 'I'll never forget the way it just dropped round her shoulders as soft and brown and easy as shit from a mare's behind. Bloody lovely it was.' He mistook my expression. 'Honest,' he repeated earnestly. His eyes closed but his own expression remained ecstatic as he apparently dozed off to sleep.

'Well, are you glad you came on the trip?' demanded Erchy from behind us.

'I wouldn't have missed it for the world,' I assured him. 'Meeting Marie and hearing all Calum's stories. It's been a wonderful evening altogether.'

'Indeed I don't know when I've enjoyed myself so much,' corroborated Behag.

'I've fairly enjoyed myself too,' Erchy admitted. 'But I'm thinkin' I'll be best pleased with it when I come to eat my dinner.' He nodded to where the box of salmon was hidden under a sack.

Behag said, 'I wonder will Calum remember to bring you the apples from that tree?'

At the mention of Calum's name Tearlaich became alert again. 'Calum?' he repeated. 'He'll not be remembering tomorrow what he's said today.'

'He has a good enough memory for some things,' I pointed out. 'All those stories he told us tonight. I loved listening to them.'

'Aye, I noticed that,' he murmured non-comittally. There was a glint in his eyes which I put down to my use of the word 'loved'. Bruachites 'like fine' something. The word 'loved' in such a context they looked upon as amusing exaggeration.

'He seemed pretty certain he'd seen those fairies, too,' I said. 'Did you believe him about that?' I taxed him.

'Believe him? What, that fellow? I'd as soon believe a drunken tinker,' he scoffed. 'Ach, you mustn't believe any story Calum tells you,' he added half seriously.

72

'Not any?' I repeated with a slight feeling of dismay.

'Not a one,' reiterated Tearlaich. 'That man!' His face broke into a broad approbatory smile. 'I'm tellin' you, Miss Peckwitt, he's the most beautiful liar God ever put two boots on.'

Family Silver

Fergus Beag (Little Fergus) had died suddenly at the age of eighty-two and, as was customary, the women of the village were calling at varying times before the burial to condole with the widow, Ina. Morag, her niece, Behag, and I went together after the chores were done and evening was beginning to soften what had been one of the summer's really hot days.

'Hector was girnin' again about him goin' so sudden,' confided Behag with a hint of apology. 'He was sayin' Fergus will be one of the heaviest corpses they've had yet to carry to the burial ground an' him havin' no illness to weaken him first.'

Little Fergus had in his prime been one of the biggest men in the village – over six foot tall and with shoulders as broad as a door. Even at eighty-two he had been no lightweight but because his father had been 'Fergus Mor' (Big Fergus) the son naturally had been dubbed 'Little Fergus' and 'Little Fergus' he had remained despite the subsequent inaptness of the description.

'Ach, Hector will soon stop his girnin' once they have the grave dug an' a good dram for their pains,' Morag comforted with a sly smile at me.

'If they ever have it dug,' murmured Behag dubiously.

Morag gave her a searching glance. 'An' why will they no'?'

'Did you not hear Hector complainin' this mornin' that his leg was troublin' him?' asked Behag.

'Which leg was that?' demanded Morag as if Hector had a selection. 'The one he left behind him in the boat when he twisted his foot?'

A baffled expression flitted across Behag's face. 'I believe that was the one,' she admitted.

'What happened?' I asked.

'Ach, Hector was steppin' out from his boat to the dinghy with his hands full of fishes,' scoffed Morag. 'He had one of his legs over the side when didn't a floorboard slip an' jam his foot under it. It was no more than if a cow had stepped on it but to hear Hector shoutin' you'd think it was on crutches he'd be for the rest of his life.'

'But his ankle was as big as a haggis for a day or two an' sore right up his leg,' defended Behag.

'But that was more than a week ago,' protested Morag.

'It was so but he was feelin' it again this mornin'. Did you not hear him sayin' that?'

'I did,' responded Morag with a grim smile. 'An' I heard Erchy swearin' he'd make sure Hector dug his share of the grave supposin' he has to stand on his head to do it.' Behag sighed acceptance.

Bruach graves were dug not by an official grave digger but by any relatives of the deceased fit enough to accomplish the task and Hector and Erchy, being Fergus Beag's two nearest male relatives in the village, had been called upon to do their duty. Erchy could always be relied upon but Hector's aversion to physical labour and his habit of developing agonising back or stomach pains or even disappearing altogether for a day or two whenever there was a chance of his being compelled to wield a spade was so well known in Bruach that even the loyal Behag was at times hard put to it to find excuses for her husband.

Our path to the late Fergus' cottage wound sinuously over the heather-covered moors and was wide enough for only two people to walk abreast so that Behag and I, who were barelegged and wearing shoes, had appropriated it for ourselves, while Morag, who persisted whatever the weather in wearing gumboots on weekdays, scuffed her way through the bristly heather, scattering drifts of moths as if she were scuffing her way through autumn leaves.

'I'm thinkin' it's no' like Fergus to die so sudden,' she observed. 'But ach, he was always the queer one right enough.'

'What took him d'you think?' asked Behag.

'His heart, likely,' returned Morag. 'The doctor was sayin' that people livin' in hilly places like this always has hearts.'

'He was a good age, after all,' I pointed out.

'Aye,' Morag allowed, 'he was a good age but indeed I never seem to mind that Fergus was ever young. Not to my way of thinkin'.'

'Why do you say that?' Behag asked.

'Well he was that religious an' that ages a man,' Morag explained. 'An' another thing, even as a child he used to have a lot of these premunitions. That always made him seem older than he was.'

'Premunitions?' echoed Behag. 'What sort of premunitions?'

'Did you never hear how he knew Old Farquhar's house was to go on fire weeks, but no, months, before it happened?' demanded Morag in an incredulous voice.

'No, I never did,' denied Behag. I also shook my head.

'Nor of him premunising the death of his daughter?'

'I did not,' said Behag, sounding as indignant as if she had been denied food at a banquet.

76

'I remember your telling me his daughter had been killed in an accident but I didn't know there'd been any warning of it beforehand,' I disclosed.

Morag was so astonished at our admissions that she stopped in her tracks, staring at us as if trying to divine some reason for our imperfect tuition. 'Well, indeed, it was so,' she reiterated as she started walking again.

'Tell us about it,' I coaxed. We still had the best part of a mile to walk and I knew from experience that if Morag would regale us with stories of past happenings in Bruach the journey would not seem half so long.

She needed little encouragement. 'Fergus an' Ina, now, they had none but this one child, Alex they used to call her. Aye, an' she was always a queer kind of lassie too, to my way of thinkin'; not what you'd expect from folks like Fergus an' Ina, for though Fergus was queer himself he was a good man for his work an' for his church. Indeed,' she added parenthetically, 'maybe she wasn't rightly Fergus' child at all for he was often away at sea an' Ina was always one for the lads. Alex grew up hatin' the croft an' wouldn't settle so she left home when she was gey young an' went to be a servant. Folks were after sayin' it was Fergus' religion that drove her away an' I doubt myself that was the reason.' She permitted herself a small sigh. 'Ach, right enough he was awful hard on the girl.'

'Did she not come home at all?' asked Behag.

'Aye, she'd come home maybe for a holiday now an' then, an' for her mother to make a great fuss of her but she never stayed long. A week or two an' then she was away again. Fergus used to grumble. A "gogaid" – that's a flighty one – he would say she was for he was wantin' she should stay an' help her mother on the croft, though she'd have none of it. As she got older she came home less an' less an' she hadn't been home for a while when one evenin', an' it was an evenin' like this one.' Morag waved an arm at the quiet moors and the lustrous sky. 'Fergus was comin' home from the moor after milkin' the cow an' suddenly he hears the sound of weepin' comin' seemingly from behind a peat stack. He goes to look but there's no sound nor sight of a thing an' he's just makin' back to the path when the weepin' begins again, only louder, an' he's sure it's his own daughter an' she pourin' her grief on to the heather. He's that upset he stands still an' calls, "Alex, is it yourself?" At that the weepin' grows fainter an' more far away till he can hear it no more.'

'An' was that when she was killed?' asked Behag, awestruck.

Morag tossed the interruption aside. 'Fergus found he was shiverin' so much he made for home as quick as he. could an' when he got inside, though it was a warm night, he piled wood an' peats on the fire till Ina thought the flames would be comin' out of the chimney an' she so hot she had to go an' sit in the door. "Whatever ails you?" she asks him. "You'll know soon enough," says he, an' gets a blanket off the bed an' wraps it round his shoulders an' sits as close to the fire as if he'd been all day at the back of the hills in a snowstorm.'

'Did he not tell Ina about hearing their daughter's voice?' This time the interruption was mine.

'He did not,' confirmed Morag. 'He told no one then, but Ina says she knew he'd had one of his premunitions to make him turn like that. Sure enough the next day there came a wire tellin' them their daughter had been killed in an accident. Then it was that Fergus told Ina what had happened to him while he was out on the moors.'

'Did they ever find out when was the accident?' Behag's tone was meek.

'They did,' replied Morag. 'An' it was just about the time Fergus must have been comin' back from the cow.' Morag turned to see how deeply her story had affected us. 'Now will you believe that!' she enjoined us.

Neither Behag nor I made any reply. Behag was the most credulous woman in Bruach and on a lonely moor in the company of Gaels I could shed logic as easily as I could shed a wet shawl.

'An' another time I mind,' continued Morag, warming to her subject. 'There was the time he was skipper of a boat for a rich man.' She paused. 'You knew he was a skipper when he was young?' she asked us. We acknowledged that this fact we did know.

'Aye well, the owner had decided they was to spend the night at moorings; strong, new moorings they were,' she emphasised, 'an' they'd cost him a deal of money gettin' them laid specially by the firm that made them. But Fergus wasn't happy. He could sense a storm comin' an' though they'd all gone to their beds an' it wasn't his turn to be on duty he couldn't seem to settle. He was that worried he went an' woke the engineer an' told him to get up a good head of steam an' keep her at the ready. Fergus said the engineer was none too pleased to be got out of his bed since everyone had been sayin' the new moorings was strong enough to hold a battleship in a hurricane, but he did as he was told. When the storm broke it wasn't such a bad one as storms at sea go but they hadn't been ridin' it more than half an hour before those strong new moorings broke just as Fergus knew they would.'

'That was a lucky one,' I murmured.

'Lucky?' echoed Morag. 'Indeed if Fergus hadn't made the man get steam up it's likely the ship an' all their lives would have been lost.'

'What did the owner have to say?' asked Behag. 'You'd have expected him to give Fergus a good pound for that.'

'Indeed the owner wouldn't believe it at first when Fergus woke him to tell him but he believed it all right afterwards when he saw it for himself. They got some divers down to inspect the moorings an' they found somethin' wrong with them that had caused them to part. Fergus said the owner took the firm who'd made them to the law over it an' won his case.'

'Did he ever ask Fergus why he'd made sure they had steam up?' I asked.

'He did,' declared Morag. 'An' when Fergus told him he shakes hands with him. "Fergus," says he, "I've always laughed at your premunitions before but I never will again." He never did an' that's the truth. He never forgot that night, either, an' when he died he left Fergus a pension for the rest of his life.'

'It's nice to hear of that,' I remarked.

'Aye, there's some of these rich folk that do right by people,' admitted Morag grudgingly.

'I wouldn't care to see the future,' said Behag with a slight shudder.

'Well, Fergus could without a doubt,' Morag told her. 'An' that's what folks will best remember him for when they're speakin' of him. Aye,' she repeated, 'they'll remember his premunitions.'

I did not divulge then it was in no supersensory way that I should best remember Fergus. I had been living with Morag for some time before starting to look around for a house and croft of my own and hearing of one which had been empty for years and might possibly be bought I set out one day to find it. I knew roughly where it was situated but I knew also that if I kept to the road it was going to be a long trek and as it was winter with short hours of daylight I took what I thought to be a short cut. Morag has assured me there was such a path but her instructions, always more colourful than correct, had led me into a deep, boggy valley. At that early stage of my initiation bogs terrified me and in mounting panic, visualising myself being sucked rapidly into miry mud with darkness coming on and no one to see my plight, I tried repeatedly to find a path back to firm ground but drew back each time as I went ankle deep in treacly mire. Common sense told me my panic was foolish. The day was mild for the time of year; the sun indicated it was around midday and except for one or two historic and easily identifiable bogs none was reputed to be dangerous except to cows and horses with their small feet and heavy bodies. All the same I was immensely relieved to see Fergus coming over the hill in my direction carrying a creel of peats. I hailed him and, still with the heavy creel on his back, he came towards me, testing the ground at every few steps. He guided me back to the path and asked me where I was making for. I told him and begged for directions.

'You've lost yourself, have you?' he said with mockery in his voice.

I grinned and acknowledged I was a little lost.

'Aye, aye, I thought that must be the way of it.' With a hand that was as hard as a cricket bat on my shoulder he turned me in the direction I was to go. He raised his right arm. 'Now look along the length of that,' he instructed. Obediently I looked along the length of his arm. 'Now you'll see that,' he went on, holding up a sturdy thumb that was as dark and wrinkled as oak bark. I assured him I could see it. 'Now, Miss Peckwitt,' he told me, wedging each word into the sentence as carefully as a mason wedging stones into a wall, 'you'll just take a line from the black of my thumbnail,' he commanded. Heedfully I had done so.

The three of us were now approaching the croft land as distinct from the moor and the ever-elusive corncrakes were croaking in the unscythed grass down towards the burn.

'I mind my father always used to say those birds made him think of the angels,' observed Morag as I stopped to listen.

I looked at her. The rasping of the corncrake might be music to the ear of an ornithologist but it was hardly what one would expect to hear from angels.

'Aye, he'd say they're all around you an' yet you scarcely ever saw one,' she explained.

When we were within a few paces of Fergus' cottage two women emerged wearing suitably staid expressions.

'How is she?' asked Morag.

'Ach, she's no' bad. No' bad at all,' replied one of the women.

'She's frettin' more about gettin' her cow to the bull before her season's over,' added the other. 'She's wonderin' if Angy will get here in time or will one of the men come an' do it for her.'

Angy, being Fergus' nephew, was now Ina's closest relative and was confidently expected to come from the mainland and take over both his great aunt and the small croft.

'He'll surely be here for the funeral,' Morag asserted. 'They'll need him for the carryin'.'

'The more the better,' agreed one of the women.

'I'm thinkin' the men will be awful dry if the weather stays as hot as this,' commented Behag.

The sombre expressions on the faces of the women were wiped off as easily as dust from a mirror as we all turned to assess a setting sun so fiery that one expected the sea's rim to hiss and bubble as they touched. The hills were clear except for a crumpled bunch of cloud behind their peak which looked as if it might have been a coverlet hastily thrown aside.

'I believe this weather will stay with us for a whiley yet,' predicted Morag with satisfaction. 'Surely carryin' Fergus is goin' to make the men sweat worse than carryin' a load of hay.' A gloating smile creased her face. 'Mind you,' she went on, 'I believe they'd as soon he died now as wait till they're busy at the hay.'

The murmurs of agreement from the two women were cut short by a croaking voice calling from inside the cottage.

'She's hearin' us,' whispered Morag. 'You two had best away an' we'll go in to her.'

Despite the warm perfection of the evening Old Ina, Fergus' widow, was sitting in a chair drawn close to the hearth, cherishing the fire as if, now that Fergus had gone, it was destined to become her mate. Behag and I settled ourselves on the bench and mumbled trite commiserations while Morag, going immediately to the old woman, laid a hand on her shoulder and crooned comfortingly in the infinitely more expressive Gaelic. Ina shook her head or nodded, making whispered denials and acquiescence and after a few minutes Morag came and sat on the bench beside us. Her voice became more matter-of-fact.

'Would you say he had a premunition about it?' she asked.

'Indeed, I'm sure now that was the way of it,' replied Ina. We leaned forward avidly. 'Aye, an' I should have known it,' continued the widow, 'for when he came in that evening for his potatoes he ate three sooyan along with them before he pushed his plate at me for more. "That's a meal enough for a ploughman you've taken already," says I. "Right enough," says he, "but I don't wish to go my way hungry." "Go?" I asks him. "Go which way?" But he doesn't say a word an' just goes through to the room an' lies on the bed an' that's the last speech I had with him till I went to tell him it was time to go to the milkin' an' found him gone.' Her voice faltered and she struck her forehead with the back of her hand.

'It's sad, mo ghaoil,' Morag sympathised when the widow had recovered herself. 'An' him such a strong healthy man all his life.'

'Indeed he was so,' agreed Ina, wiping the sleeve of her cardigan across her eyes.

'An' always so good to eat,' prompted Morag.

'Good to eat an' good to sleep,' the widow confirmed.

'An' never seein' a doctor.'

'He saw a doctor only once in these twenty years past,' Ina replied, 'an' that was only to see how he was wearin'.'

'Aye, aye,' commented Morag. 'An' nothin' artificial about him,' she added.

'Nothin' but his teeths,' corrected Ina.

'Did he have his teeths?' Morag's voice was sharp with surprise. 'I never saw them, then.'

'Indeed they never came out of that little box you see there on the chimney shelf,' confided the widow. 'Never once but when he took them out to polish them.' I glanced up at the exquisite little lacquered box which sat between what I had discovered on a previous visit to Ina to be a Georgian silver salt-cellar and pepper-shaker.

'He polished them?' asked Morag with a touch of scepticism.

'He did so. The same time as he polished the other ornaments there with some stuff he got from the van. There should be a tin of it there now.' She indicated a tin of a well-known brand of metal polish which stood tied in a duster at the end of the mantelpiece. 'He liked to see things shine,' she explained. 'I daresay it was the boat in him still.'

Ina picked up a pair of tongs roughly fashioned out of fencing wire and added a couple of peats to the fire.

'You'll take a cup of tea,' she stated with shaky-voiced emphasis and shifted the kettle from the hob to the hook above the fire. While the kettle boiled and the other three

84

women talked pious trivialities I studied Ina's kitchen with its wood walls tanned by peat smoke; its bare wood floor dark as lichen with age and wear. Apart from the long wooden bench on which we sat there were two roughly made upright chairs, a table obviously knocked up from driftwood and a varnished dresser which occupied almost the whole of the wall opposite the window. The lower shelves of the dresser were loaded with plain earthenware basins of uniform size; brown glazed jugs of varying sizes, and an assortment of stone jam jars, while on the top shelf sat three fat brown teapots interspersed with such oddments as a pewter tankard, sporting an engraved coat of arms; a silver sauce-boat, and one of a pair of elegant silver candlesticks. The last time I had been in Ina's house both candlesticks had been on display, as had also a pair of silver meat-dish covers which had hung on the wall on either side of the dresser.

'Useless things!' Ina had said when I had admired them. I glanced about me, trying to locate the missing items, and soon found the candlestick which was propping open the tiny window to allow the slight evening breeze to drift into the over-warm room. The meat-dish covers I could see nowhere and I sighed for Ina's indifference to her treasures, wondering if Morag's 'anticsman' had paid her a visit or if some travelling tinker had cast a covetous eye on them and had exchanged them for a couple of milk pails or even tin water dippers. It was so unusual to see such treasures in a crofter's kitchen that I had once asked Morag how the old woman had come by them, imagining that perhaps Ina was descended from some once wealthy family and these were the remaining heirlooms or perhaps that at some time in her youth she had acquired a taste for fine things and had saved up her money and bought them on rare visits to the mainland. Admittedly neither theory fitted Ina's present attitude towards her valuables but that could always be put down to age or the bludgeoning effect of a harsh crofting life.

'An' hasn't she a box full of other things under her bed in the room?' demanded Morag. 'Dishes an' spoons an' little ornaments, all wrapped in pieces of blanket. She showed them to me one time.'

'It seems so odd,' I began, but Morag cut me short.

'Ach, Ina doesn't know they're valuable,' she said. 'Nobody's told her an' it's best if no one does.'

'Why ever not?' I asked, puzzled.

'Well, you see, mo ghaoil, when Ina's daughter was alive she used to travel about the country takin' jobs as a servant in these big houses. She never seemed to stay in any place for long but she was always sendin' her mother home some little keepsake or other. Ina thought she was buyin' them an' sendin' them for her to keep till the girl got married.'

'Oh,' I said expressively.

'Aye,' agreed Morag. 'So there they are an' where they rightly belong the Dear only knows but it's certain it's not in Ina's kitchen or under her bed.'

The tea was brewed, the girdle scones handed round. Ina was not eating and Morag began questioning the old woman as to what food she had taken that day.

Ina shook her head. 'I have no hunger,' she said.

'That's no way to be,' Morag told her severely. 'Wait you now while I just switch you up an egg in a bitty milk an' supposin' you take nothin' else till the mornin' you'll not starve.' Bending down she extracted a pan from under the dresser and poured in some milk from the pail. She peered in various basins.

'Where do you keep your eggs?' She turned to Ina.

'Indeed if there's none in the basin there's none in the house,' replied Ina. 'I mind now I didn't gather them yet today,' she added plaintively.

'Did you feed your hens?' enquired Morag.

'Kirsty did that for me while she was here,' admitted Ina.

I volunteered to go to the henhouse to look for eggs.

'You'll take this an' see an' just lift the clocky hens while you're at it,' said Ina, showing signs of animation. From beside the fireplace she picked up a bowl of meal in which reposed a long-handled serving ladle. 'You'll just lift up the hens an' throw them into the air,' she instructed me. 'They've been sittin' that tight the last four or five days an' they're needin' to come off or they'll get stuck.'

I assured her I knew how to deal with broody hens and, picking up the basin and ladle, went out towards the henhouse, casually inspecting the ladle on my way. It was heavy and dull but as I had expected the hall marks on the handle were plainly visible.

There was a cluster of hens outside the henhouse all obviously questioning and counselling one another as to whether it was time to go and roost. I shooed them aside and bending down entered the tiny, strong-smelling shed where the two clocky hens sat, screened by pieces of sacking, one at either side in nests only slightly raised from the floor. The first hen tried to peck me as I lifted her out and when I threw her into the air she came down with such a squalling and shrieking that the rest of the hens scattered in panic. The second clocky reacted similarly and I watched until they had muted which was what was required of them and then threw down ladles of food, fending off the other hens until the clockies had eaten their fill. Only then did I go back into the henhouse and after collecting the eggs from half a dozen laying boxes I crouched down to check that there were no broken hatching eggs in the two snug hay-lined nests near the floor. The neat shape of the nests intrigued me and pulling aside a little of the hay to inspect them I found my fingernail was scratching on metal. I lifted a little more hay, then sat back on my heels, shaken with a mixture of disbelief and laughter. I had found the two silver meat-dish covers. They were tarnished and speckled with excreta but undoubtedly they made excellent nests for the two clocky hens and their expected progeny.

Wild Wander

I awoke with the first flurry of wind around the house and lay drowsily listening and wondering if this was just an exploratory thrust of a breeze attendant upon the turn of the tide or whether it was in the nature of a rehearsal for a gale which, gaining proficiency, would stampede the calm spell that had been lulling us during the past few days. The flurry died briefly then came again, still indecisive. I tried to guess at the time. It had been day bright when I had gone to bed at my usual time and it was day bright now and I felt as if I had slept no more than an hour. I gave up guessing and stretched out an arm to pick up the alarm clock. It was a crippled clock; both its feet had gone so that it had to lie prone and the minute hand had broken off, but as nearly all Bruach clocks were either crippled or wildly eccentric I saw no reason to waste money on a new one. Except for the postmistress, the schoolteacher and the bus driver 'mechanical time' was of little importance. In winter, day began with the very first glimmer of light which told the mothers of school-age children that there was time only for them to make a quick bowl of brose and murmur a bible reading before rushing the children off to school. It told the rest of us that though there might be time for a more leisurely breakfast this must be followed by a few brief hours crammed with disciplined comings and goings; carrying hay for the outwintered cattle; milking;

mucking out and renewing bedding; bringing water from the well and peats from the stack; feeding hens, and yet more hay carrying until it was dark and we could recuperate with a long evening beside the fire until one decided for oneself that it was time for the day to end. During the spring and early summer when nights were transient enough to pass almost unnoticed the working day was not so easily definable. The children took their cue for school by the smoke which appeared from the schoolhouse chimney (the peat fire burned all the year round) and their mothers knew it was time to put on the potatoes for the evening meal when the returning scholars were sighted climbing the homeward path, but though these two daily events served as useful reminders to the rest of us no one appeared to notice the lack of them when the school was closed for the holidays. We would say, 'It is time to milk the cows', or, 'It is time to feed the hens', or, 'It is time to take my dinner', and even I, novice that I was, rarely glanced at a clock for guidance. Time became instinctive: a sense that developed with the constant observation of the sky and sun shadows and the behaviour of animals and birds whose promptings were less arbitrary and more reliable than clocks and watches.

Confused now by sleep I stared at the clock. The hour hand had crept fractionally past four showing me that it was some three hours before my usual waking time. My body felt as if it was roped to the bed with the need for sleep but nevertheless I continued listening, trying to gauge the strength of the wind and almost whimpering a prayer that it would die away for just three or four hours so that I could finish my rest when, I promised, it could blow for weeks and I should not grumble. Since coming to live in Bruach I had found I was inclined to sleep less deeply on nights of calm and quiet than on nights of bustling storm, wind and rain being the characteristic pattern of our weather and calm spells merely an interruption. Like everyone else I rejoiced in the respite from the interminable battles with the wind but I was conscious that if they lasted more than a day or two they became seductive, luring me into negligence. Perhaps into leaving an empty wheelbarrow out on the croft; into forgetting a feeding bowl or some garden tool that a strong gust could snatch up and hurl against a window; into omitting the extra tie on a barn door which, if the door were blown open, could result in the loss of the roof and though I might go to bed happily exhausted by all the extra work the calm spell had enabled me to accomplish there was always this subconscious awareness of more elementary chores neglected so that I was inclined to sleep fitfully, one ear alert for the first threatening rushes of a rising wind.

The flurries were undoubtedly gaining strength, punching at the windows and the roof. A pail rattled over the cobblestones and a tub went bumping after it reminding me of yesterday's big wash of sheets still on the clothes-line. I jumped out of bed and slid into some clothes. As soon as I opened the door I could hear the noise of the sheets cracking like whips as they streamed in the wind and I hastened to rescue them. Some of the pegs had gone and the hems were already beginning to fray with long cottons plagued into tangles but I was relieved to see they were still whole. Once before when I had been slow to take in sheets left out in a gale I had found only the top hems still pegged to the clothes-line; the rest were white remnants clinging to clumps of spiky heather and decorating the barbed wire and netting fence around the haystack. At that time it had been a near disaster since my linen cupboard was not well stocked and I was expecting a succession of visitors. My only recourse had been to buy sheets from 'Aberdeen Angus', the cheerful Asian tinker, whose entire stock I discovered to have become stained

91

along the folds with a most persistent brown dye which had leaked from the cheap and inevitably sodden portmanteaus in which he always carried round his wares.

As soon as I grasped the sheets the remaining pegs flew out and I fought the wind for possession of my bundle, crushing it against me as I trotted back to the house. Dumping it on the table I sped back to the croft, retrieving anything that might be blown away: a bundle of potato sacks washed in the burn and left to dry on the stone dyke; odd pieces of driftwood; a half-gallon tin of paint which I had been using to paint the barn door; a shovel; a broom, and a couple of pails. Even a creel of peats had to be taken to the safety of the shed since it had already been nudged over and some of the peats scattered thus making the creel light enough to be tumbled about and perhaps become airborne should the wind increase to a gale. Satisfied at last I returned to the cottage and while I folded the sheets, cool and fresh-smelling as the dawn wind itself, I debated whether it was worth while going back to bed. My sorties into the brisk morning had driven away the yearning for sleep and I wondered whether after a quick cup of coffee I should turn my back on work and make the most of the enforced early rising by indulging in what I liked to call a 'wild wander'. Several times during the kindlier months of the year I liked to make these early-morning expeditions either along the shore or over the moors before there was much risk of other people being about and rarely did I return without the reward of having glimpsed some shy, wild creature or witnessed a thrilling example of animal behaviour the memory of which I knew would remain with me for the rest of my life. I had seen the elusive wild cat slinking among the bracken; I had observed at close quarters a family of otters playing like puppies at the mouth of a cave until, presumably winding me, they slid lithe as snakes across the rocks and into the sea. I had come at low tide within forty yards of a party of seals, lying out on the rocks and rolling and flopping their great bodies into first one position and then another while they expressed their satisfaction or otherwise by noises that were half belches, half groans. I had been puzzled by a gathering of weasels, I counted seven in all, which appeared to be playing a game of 'In and out of the bluebells' on a mossy bank near the shore, and I had watched enchanted while a magnificent stag had led his party of hinds across a swollen burn, turning every now and then it seemed to reassure the more apprehensive among them. At almost any time there was a variety of wild life to be observed in and around Bruach but in the early mornings when it felt as if the day itself had only just begun to breathe there was more chance of surprising the more wily or more timid creatures which, once discerning the slightest stir of human activity, speedily retreated to the security of the hills or took refuge on unscaleable cliffs. Admittedly there were mornings when I saw nothing more unusual than a stag silhouetted against the skyline; a buzzard swooping on a rabbit, or a patient heron being attacked by a couple of gulls which coveted his fresh-caught breakfast, but no matter how common the sight for me the wonder and the rapture were always there. I had come straight to Bruach from the town and though the ensuing years had moulded me into a countrywoman they had not lessened my excitement on seeing creatures of the wild. So far as they were concerned I knew I should remain in a perpetual state of wonder.

I opened the door and studied the great soft clouds that were moving serenely across the sky to join those already in ambush behind the hills. With this wind I should have expected them to be racing across the sky and I seemed to recollect that according to Bruach weather lore when there was 'more wind low than high' it was a sign that the wind would not last long. The morning was inviting. I made my cup of coffee and refused to think of work. As yet I could see no threat of rain in the sky but all the same I pulled on an oilskin, tied it round my waist with a length of rope and pushed a sou'wester into the pocket. In Bruach it was usually raining, had just ceased raining or was threatening to rain so it was as well to be prepared. In any case there was nothing so good as an oilskin for defence against the wind. Discarding my heavy workaday gumboots I slipped into a pair of shiny, thin-soled rubber boots, bought in an English town and kept exclusively for 'wild wanders'. Ordinary gumboots had to be heavyweight to withstand the rough stony ground and had to be several sizes too big to allow for heavy socks in winter which resulted in their clumping noisily as one walked, warning anything within a hundred yards of one's approach, but these lightweight boots, though I could feel every pebble through the thin soles, were excellent in that they kept my feet dry and yet trod as quietly as a pair of tennis pumps. Slinging my binoculars round my neck I closed the door and stood once more to assess the weather and decide which way I should go. The tide was well in and throwing great plumes of spray, wetter than any rain, over the shore so I made for the moors. As I passed the hen-run the hens came racing towards me with an expectancy that changed to puzzled murmurings as I ignored them. A feed at this hour of the morning would have upset their routine and might have affected their egg-laying. They would have to wait until I returned in about three hours' time. Crossing the stepping stones of the burn I climbed into the wind and followed one of the sheep-tracks that would take me around the shoulder of the hill and eventually into a small corrie where I could peer down into a vast chasm of tumbled rocks, reputed to be a favourite haunt of hill foxes. In all my years in Bruach I had never glimpsed a hill fox, yet I was constantly hearing the shepherd grumbling at the number of sheep they took and hearing the gamekeeper boast of the number he had shot. The shepherd claimed that hill foxes were far wilier than other foxes and described almost with admiration how one of them had got the better of him at lambing time. The shepherd had gone to check up on his ewes and found one in a sheltered corrie all by herself with newly born twin lambs. He noticed that the ewe seemed agitated and looking round for the reason soon spotted the fox stealing towards her. The ewe turned to face her enemy, backing away and trying to keep her lambs behind her but it was obvious that one of the lambs was much weaker than the other. Before the shepherd could get near enough to do anything about it the fox had nipped in and taken the weaker lamb. The shepherd scrambled quickly down into the corrie, throwing stones and shouting at the fox until it dropped its catch and made off, but he was too late. When he reached the lamb it was already dead. Just as he made his discovery he heard a sharp bleat from the ewe and turning round was in time to see the same fox slinking rapidly out of sight with the remaining lamb in its jaws. It had merely circled the corrie and while his back was turned had swiftly taken the other lamb. 'If only,' the shepherd chided himself, 'I'd had the sense to let it get away with the weaker lamb I would have been able to get the strong one to safety, but ach, he was just too clever for me I doubt.'

The shepherd told too of his experience with an old dog fox. He had been out on the hills one day looking for white heather for some friends of his and feeling rather warm he took off his jacket and left it on a small knoll while he made his way down to the burn for a drink. Having refreshed himself he was about to retrace his path to the knoll when looking up he saw the old dog fox was there pawing at something. Realising it was his own jacket he shouted and waved his arms at the fox trying to scare it off but the animal only looked at him before resuming his attack on the jacket, pulling it about the knoll until the shepherd was afraid it would be torn. He hurried forward to rescue it and just as he reached the knoll he saw the fox extract a bar of chocolate from one of the pockets. It gave him another leisurely look before loping away with the chocolate still held in its mouth. 'The look that beast gave me as it went off with my chocolate was kind of uncanny,' he used to add when he told the story.

For another mile or so I trudged on, disturbing nothing more exciting than a flock of drowsy sheep and a trio of hill ponies contentedly grazing the short grass while the wind combed their long manes. The ponies pranced away, full of summer energy and sweet mountain grass. It was while I was negotiating a skin-tight little path between two bastions of cliff which led to a miniature plaeau that I came upon the wild goats. Several times previously I had glimpsed the goats but never at such close quarters and from the concealment of the cliffs I was able to observe them without their seeing me. The herd was clustered around the entrance to a cave, the old grey billy to the fore but still fast asleep lying half curled with his nose resting on his flank like a dog. Behind him two young nannies stood steadily cudding and staring out at the sea with tranquil yellow eyes. Behind them again three more elderly nannies lay with the relaxed air of those who are enjoying a morning lie-in while two leggy kids sniffed at each other's ears and seemed to be consulting with each other as to whether they should lie down again with their elders or begin the day's gambolling.

It was said in Bruach that this herd of goats were the descendants of domesticated animals left behind by the crofters during the terrible evictions of the last century when homes and possessions were burned and pillaged by avaricious landlords but whatever their history the goats looked wild enough now with their strong horns and their long shaggy coats so matted and bramble-threaded that the wind could scarcely hustle a way through. I edged back along the path, not wishing to disturb them, and clambered up a rocky gully which brought me to an even loftier sheep-track so that when I came out at last above the corrie I had to slide and scramble down into it. I approached the rock edge cautiously expecting a snatch of wind to buffet me as I came into the open, but I was pleasantly surprised. I had been too engrossed to notice how the wind was dropping and now as I looked towards the sea I realised it was only a stiff breeze that was turning the white bellies of the waves towards the wink of silver above the mainland hills and that the gale I had prepared for would prove to be no more than a morning prank. I lay down, peering hopefully into the deep abyss, impressed as always by the sheer desolation and size of the havoc of barren rocks severed so cleanly from the rest of the land by steep, sharp cliffs that provided footholds for nothing larger than a raven. It was an eerie place and if it was true that there were many fox earths among the boulders I imagined the foxes would continue to live there without fear of molestation.

For about an hour I lay there enjoying the solitude and silence while ranging the abyss hopefully with my binoculars, without once detecting even a suggestion of movement. Any foxes were either still asleep or already out prospecting for their breakfast. I gave up, aware that I was hungry for my own breakfast and that even if I hurried by the time I reached home again my poultry would be protesting that their feed was overdue. Not wishing to risk meeting or disturbing the wild goats I began to climb, zig-zagging my way towards the higher track through mossy gullies that provided easy footholds and over projecting boulders which did not. I was standing on a ledge of rock about to pull myself up and over it when glancing carelessly to my right something caught my eye. Instinctively I froze. For a fleeting second I imagined the tawny, gold shape perched on the plinth of rock above me to be headless but as my excited thoughts steadied I realised I was looking at an enormous golden eagle standing with its head turned away from me and tucked under its wing. It looked to be about three feet high and except for the golden feathers on its back which were being gently lifted by the breeze it was as still as a carving. I gaped at it, astounded by its size and by the great talons, bigger than my own hand, which gripped the rock and I think I forgot to breathe for so long that I must eventually have let out a gasp. At any rate, some noise I made disturbed the eagle which turned its head quickly and looked straight at me with piercing yellow eyes. 'You beauty!' I raved silently. 'You stupendous, unbelievable beauty!' My heart thumped as we stared at each other with what seemed like equal incredulity until the eagle spread its great wings, poised itself for a second and without haste allowed the wind to lift it from its perch. I wanted to cry out to it to stay but I could only stand dumbly watching its trance-like descent on the wind out towards the sea where, levelling off and still without discernible movement of its magnificent wings, it glided on and on until it merged into the mainland hills and no matter how much I peered I could see it no more.

I pulled myself on to the ledge and walked to where the eagle had stood. I counted only five of my paces. It was staggering! I had actually stood within five paces of a golden eagle and I wanted to scream the fact into the wind if only to convince myself it was really true. I stood leaning against the rock, overwhelmed by my phenomenal good luck and conscious of the deep soul-satisfying elation that filled me and would, I knew, surge through me whenever I recollected my morning's adventures. 'People will never believe me,' I thought and with something of a shock realised that this was perfectly true. No one would believe me. If I mentioned my experience to my neighbours they would undoubtedly appear to accept my story but I knew myself it would sound too implausible. To have got within fifty paces of a resting golden eagle they might just have accepted but a claim to have got within five they would have regarded as pure exaggeration. It would be better to say nothing, I thought, and tried to make the thought a resolution, reminding myself that there were idiots with guns in Bruach who were the avowed enemies of eagles because of their reputation for taking new-born lambs. 'Say nothing,' I told myself firmly as I left the place of the eagle's perch. 'Say nothing,' I repeated to myself again and again. And all the time I was bursting with the urge to tell somebody. Just one other person if only to see their reaction.

Once safely past the goats' cave I dropped down again to the lower path and as I reached the corrie where I had encountered the hill ponies I saw a figure in cap and oilskins seated comfortably on a boulder and staring out to sea through binoculars. I recognised Donald, Bruach's shyest bachelor, and would have skirted the corrie so as to keep out of his way had he not appeared to sense my presence the moment I spotted him. Perhaps for a space I had been visible on the skyline while I was on the high path and he had expected me to make for the corrie. He turned and we greeted each other with stiff smiles.

'You're out early,' he observed.

I was surprised. He had always evaded addressing me directly and I had gained the impression he resented me as an intruder in Bruach. This morning, however, he appeared distinctly affable so I told him what had led me to take such an early-morning walk.

'Ach, but that was what we call a tide wind, just,' he replied, confirming what by this time I already knew. 'Even this bitty breeze will be away before the tide's been gone back for more than an hour.' He looked up at me. 'You'd best be tryin' to learn the ways of the wind.'

I gave a rueful little laugh. 'I try,' I told him, 'and I know more of its ways now than when I first came to Bruach but these, what you call "tide winds", usually manage to fox me.' His expression became faintly superior. 'You're out early yourself,' I observed.

'Aye.' He rose deliberately. 'I'd best be away back to my house or the cailleach will be shoutin' I'm starvin' her hens.' Donald lived with his testy, chair-bound old mother and did all the housework and cooking as well as the croft work. He seemed disposed to accept my company for the walk home and for once I was at a loss to know whether I should attempt to start a conversation or whether he would prefer it if we continued on our way virtually in silence. For a time I left the initiative to him although I wanted to talk to him very much. Apart from the fact that Donald was supposed to know more than anyone else about the wild life of the area I wanted to ask him why, when he had the reputation of being by far the best shot in the village, he had suddenly and without explanation put away his gun and taken to using binoculars and a camera to observe wild life rather than to destroy it indiscriminately as he once had. He bent, picked up a pebble, and aimed it at a clump of heather below the path. A surprised rabbit peered above the clump and loped unhurriedly away. Donald grunted.

'Did you know it was there?' I asked him.

'I didn't know for sure but I felt as if there should be one there.' He darted a glance at me. 'If you'd had a gun now that would have made a dinner for you.'

'I don't shoot,' I told him.

'No, I don't myself now.'

'Not at all?' I queried.

'Ach, I might get a rabbit if they're takin' too much of the corn or if the cailleach takes a fancy for one but I scarcely ever take the gun down from the wall now.'

'And yet people tell me you are easily the best shot in Bruach,' I encouraged.

'Aye, I believe I might have been once,' he acknowledged. He tweaked a stalk of grass from beside the path and stuck it in his mouth. I thought it signified the end of the subject but after we had walked another little distance in silence he turned to me, slowing his pace almost to a standstill.

'There was a time once when I'd shoot at almost anythin' that moved: rabbits, hares, grouse, hoodies, gulls, ach, any bird you'd name an' just think myself the fine fellow that I had the skill to do it but then the day came, an' it came all of a sudden, that I was brought to my senses. I grew up as you might say.'

He flushed and his yellow uneven teeth were bared in an embarrassed smile but he was still walking slowly. I reasoned that if he wanted me not to pursue the subject he would have quickened his pace again so I prompted: 'You say the day came quite suddenly?'

'Aye.' He took the stalk of grass from his mouth and started to pull it into tiny pieces between his fingers. 'Did you ever see a newly dead grouse?' he asked, looking at me searchingly.

'Yes.'

'An' did you ever notice the markings on its feathers; all its feathers, I mean, not just the wings an' the brighter coloured ones?' He moved his fingers as if he were riffling them through the feathers on a bird's breast.

'Not specially,' I confirmed.

He nodded. 'I'd shot this grouse one day an' I was just bendin' down to pick it up when suddenly the sun comes through the clouds like a pointing finger an' a wee breeze tickled at the bird's feathers, liftin' them so that it made me notice the markin's on them. Beautiful it was, beautiful just. No man could have made a thing like it. I've never been able to explain it, least of all to myself, but it was as though somethin' was behind my shoulder forcin' me to see what I'd been blind to before an' what a fearful waste it was to destroy it. I took home the grouse an' we ate it but for the first time in my life I didn't enjoy it an' when I came to put the feathers at the back of the fire an' I saw their lovely patterns goin' up in smoke I knew I didn't want to destroy another living creature. I cleaned the gun that night an' I put it up on the wall an' I doubt I've taken it down more than two or maybe three times since an' that's a good few years back.' His pace quickened. 'Ach, I daresay I was daft but that's the way of it just.'

I tried to give him an understanding smile but he kept his face averted. All the same I knew now that here was someone with whom I could safely share my secret.

'I don't suppose you'll believe me,' I began, trying to keep the excitement out of my voice, 'but up there on the crag I've just stood within five paces of a golden eagle. It was asleep with its head under its wing.'

He turned to face me. 'Why wouldn't I believe you?' he demanded. There was a wry twist to his mouth.

'Oh, it just sounds too impossible. I'd decided not to mention it at all but I was dying to tell someone. You won't let it go any further, will you?' I asked hastily. There was something about the tightening of his lips that made it unnecessary for him to answer.

'Indeed not long before you found me I was watchin' a golden eagle makin' over towards the mainland. Likely it would be the one you disturbed.'

'Oh, yes!' I exclaimed, glad of some corroboration of my story.

'You were lucky all the same,' he congratulated me. 'There's not more than one other person hereabouts that I mind ever got that close to an eagle.'

'You know of someone else?' I asked tensely.

'Aye, an' he was my own father.'

'Your father?'

'Indeed. He was salmon watchin' at the time, livin' in the bothy, an' he was comin' over to collect some fresh milk an' food. It was about midday, an' sunny an' calm. Seein' he was keepin' an eye open for his sheep at the same time he didn't stay on the path. He climbed up to a crag an' found himself almost on a level with the eagle an' so close he could touch it. Like the one you saw it had it's head under its wing so that it didn't see him. My father was a very honest man, you understand, Miss Peckwitt?' He looked at me and I nodded. 'There's nothin' that upset him more than bein' disbelieved but all the same he knew if he came back to the village tellin' nothin' but the truth about what he'd seen people wouldn't be able to bring themselves to believe him just. So, quick as a flash he slipped off his jacket an' threw it over the eagle an' held it in his arms. He lifted it an' carried it all the way down to the village an' there he started shoutin' for folks to come an' see what he had. When he thought there was enough witnesses he lifted his jacket off the eagle an' let it go.' He grinned. 'They had to believe him then.'

'He must have been even closer than I was,' I remarked.

'Aye, but I doubt you wouldn't have had the strength to carry it back even supposin' you were able to throw your jacket over it,' he replied. 'They're big birds with some weight in them.'

I laughed. 'It wouldn't have occurred to me to try,' I retorted. 'It looked enormous and its talons were really fearsome.'

He grunted again. 'You'd best be careful who you mention the eagle to,' he warned. 'There's one or two here would be out with the gun if they heard of it.'

'I've already decided I'm going to keep quiet about it,' I assured him. 'It's enough that I've seen it.'

We were coming in sight of the village now and he began to move away, gradually making for a track that would take him to the far moor gate. I guessed that he had no wish to be seen in my company.

'Aye, well,' he said, throwing the words over his shoulder, 'I'd best go an' make some breakfast.'

'D'you know,' I told him, 'I recall feeling quite hungry for my breakfast before I saw the eagle but since then the thought of food hasn't crossed my mind.'

He paused and looked at me with a gentle understanding smile.

'Ach, Miss Peckwitt,' he pronounced, 'when anyone has seen such a sight as you have seen this morning they have had food and drink for the day.' He turned his back on me and we went our separate ways.

Pears in Brine

'Well, that's us near ready,' announced Erchy, indicating the forty or so lobster creels spread on the cobbled ground at the side of the house. 'This is the last one.' He was tying a flat stone to a creel bottom and beside him sat Hector expertly plying a netting needle which, being a sedentary occupation, was the only one he cared to undertake.

'When Hector's finished that net we'll have forty-two creels for tarrin' tomorrow an' if the weather holds they'll be in the water by Wednesday surely.'

'It's a pity you have to put in the stones before you net them,' I said, lifting one of the creels. 'It makes them terribly heavy to carry.' I picked up another creel. 'Two of them balance quite well, though,' I observed, weighing one against the other. 'Would you like me to take these two down to the shore for you, seeing I'm going down anyway.'

I thought Erchy was about to refuse my offer but Hector interrupted quickly. 'Aye, let her,' he said magnanimously. 'It'll be two less for us to carry.'

'Aye.' Erchy's voice was dubious. 'So long as she doesn't fall an' break them.' He finished tying the stone. 'Where did you put your own creel?' he asked me.

I nodded towards the house. 'Beside the door,' I told him.

105

'Aye, well you'd best fetch it here. I'll be ready to sort it for you just now.'

I brought him my one creel which he had promised to mend for me. He inspected it with a disgruntled air. 'Ach, you'd best have a new creel. This one is like matchwood.'

'It will do me,' I argued, knowing that if this one was not repaired I should be without a creel for the rest of the season and I dearly fancied a fresh lobster.

Erchy sat down and began tearing off the old net which was like a ravel of dirty string.

'If you boys hasn't got your creels in the sea yet you'd be best leavin' them on the shore!' Angy, who had forsaken his job as a fisherman to come and take over the deceased Fergus' croft, appeared from the direction of the house. He was a small man with a thin, bouncy figure, red hair and sea-blue eyes. He looked at my creel. 'You're surely not thinkin' of puttin' that in the water?' he asked contemptuously. 'Surely the lobster would be walkin' in an out of it as if it was its own kitchen.'

'That's what I've been sayin' to her myself,' agreed Erchy. 'But she's that thrawn. She'll no' listen.'

Hector smiled impishly. 'You'd best be careful what you're sayin',' he jested. 'She might be catchin' more wiss her one than us wiss our forty.'

'Indeed an' that will be the way of it unless we get ours into the water pretty soon,' returned Erchy.

I ought to have left them to their work and their chat but Erchy's mother had made me promise to await her return from the well so that she could give me a pat of homemade butter for my supper and it was pleasant outside in the silky breeze with the bright sun gentled by drifts of clouds that looked soft and white as a rabbit's belly.

'Are you tarrin' them here or down at the shore?' asked Angy.

'On the shore,' Erchy replied.

Hands in pockets, cigarette in the side of his mouth, Angy studied the assembled creels. 'How will you get this lot down anyway? You'll need to hire a lorry.'

'We're hirin' no lorry,' retorted Erchy.

'You'll surely not be thinkin' of carryin' them down yourself?' Angy, having been a professional fisherman, was inclined to be scornful of Bruach's part-timers. 'You'll need help if you are.'

'We're carryin' them down but we'll have help all right.' There was a combative look in Erchy's eyes.

'I'm taking two on my way home,' I interpolated. 'And I expect there'll be others willing.'

'I'm no meanin' that sort of help,' exclaimed Erchy. 'What we'll do is wait till it gets a wee bit dark an' then we'll take the bier from the church an' carry them down on that.'

'The funeral bier?' I echoed.

'Aye,' affirmed Erchy, 'it will hold a good few creels at a time will that.'

'People won't like it,' I pointed out.

'Why should they complain?' asked Erchy. 'It's not as if we're tarrin' the creels first. Right enough I wouldn't think it right to get the bier all covered in tar,' he added virtuously.

Angy's eyes sparkled. He was already beginning to get the reputation of being a practical joker and now he nodded appreciatively. 'By God! I wish I'd thought of that myself,' he said.

'I'm sure some people are going to be offended,' I repeated.

'Not more than a couple of fresh lobsters will cure,' declared Erchy confidently. He turned to me. 'You'd best not let on you know anythin', all the same,' he warned.

'Just keep your eyes an' your door tight shut if you hear some strange noises near the place tonight.'

'You're aimin' to take them down this night?' asked Angy.

'We are so,' responded Erchy. 'We're meanin' to spend the day tarrin' them tomorrow.'

Angy looked downcast. 'You're not wantin' the job I spoke about, then?'

'We are not,' replied Erchy. 'Like you said, if we don't get these creels into the water soon we're as well leavin' them ashore.' His voice became emphatic. 'We're tarrin' them tomorrow an' puttin' them into the sea the next day if we're spared. There'll be no time to do any job save that.'

'There'll be good money in it,' said Angy persuasively.

At the mention of money Hector evinced a mild interest in the conversation. 'How much?' he asked.

'Ach, I couldn't say for sure, but plenty. The family's rich enough anyway.'

'How would you know that?' demanded Erchy.

'They must be,' asserted Angy. 'They pay income tax anyway.'

Hector enveloped the three of us in his broad guileful smile. 'If tsey pay income tax tsey must be daft as well as rich, I'm tsinkin',' he commented.

'I cannot see why the boat you were on yourself doesn't drop it off,' suggested Erchy. 'Do they not pass near to the island most every day?'

'With herrin' the price it is how would they take time off from the fishin' just to deliver a corpse?' argued Angy. 'Anyway, fishermen don't take to coffins aboard their boats. They say it brings bad luck.'

'An' aren't we expectin' to be fishermen?' responded Erchy.

Angy hastily pushed another cigarette between his lips. 'Not herrin' fishermen, you're not,' he replied. 'I believe

108

corpses only affect herrin'. I don't believe the lobsters mind them at all.'

I had pricked up my ears at the mention of a corpse but deemed it wiser to ask no questions and there was an appreciable silence before anyone spoke again.

'It would set us back wiss tse creels, right enough,' remarked Hector. 'We'd need a good pound for tsat.'

'Well, I'm gettin' nothin' out of it,' said Angy off-handedly. 'I only said I'd ask you seein' they weren't findin' it easy to get a boat an' I thought you'd be keen on the money.'

'Not that keen,' muttered Erchy.

'Ach, then, I'll away to the Post Office an' telephone to say you're not comin', will I?' said Angy.

At that moment Erchy's mother returned and I went with her into the house. When I left there was no sign of any of the three men but the next morning Hector and Erchy's boat had gone from its moorings and the untarred creels were piled in a mound on the shore.

'Where have they gone?' I asked Morag.

'Ach, they're away to take a corpse to one of the islands, though the Dear knows why,' she replied.

'I heard them discussing it yesterday and they seemed determined they weren't going to take it,' I told her.

'They were not indeed but, ach, I think it was the money tempted them in the end,' she explained.

Later in the day whilst I was repairing the stone dyke which surrounded my cottage I was surprised to see a fishing boat come into the bay and drop anchor. The sound of a klaxon horn hit the village followed some time later by the noise of booted feet clumping down the brae. It was Angy and I guessed that this was the boat on which he had worked. I watched him row out and climb aboard.

'You're a hardy!' Behag's voice startled me momentarily and one of my carefully placed stones rolled out of position.

'That's Angy's friends come for a ceilidh with him,' she enlightened me, shielding her eyes as she studied the boat. Under her arm Behag had the new skirt which she wished me to 'gather her in round the middle' so I left my dyke-mending and went with her back to the cottage where she slipped out of her old skirt and tried on the new one. I was just pinning in some darts when we heard heavy footsteps approaching.

'Who can it be?' gasped Behag and sooner than risk having her skirt fall down and despite all the pins I had inserted she promptly sat on the nearest chair, pulling her jersey well down over her waistline. Angy stood in the doorway.

'It's my mates that was,' he explained after the preliminary greetings had been exchanged. 'They're sayin' all their bread's gone mouldy on them an' they're thinkin' maybe they'd get a loaf from you. Just what will do them till mornin' when they'll be back in port.'

'They've no bread at the shop,' interjected Behag. 'I was up there this mornin' an' there's none till the bus comes this evenin'.'

'Ach, you wouldn't expect the shop to have bread at this time of day,' scoffed Angy.

'I've no bread either,' I told him. 'But I've plenty of oatcakes and it won't take me a minute to bake them some girdle scones.'

'Aye, that will do them fine,' Angy accepted and sat down to wait.

I heated the girdle over the fire and tipped flour into a basin. 'Behag,' I said, 'will you brew the tea? The kettle is boiling and I daresay Angy will be glad of a cup.' She did not move and when I glanced at her enquiringly I saw she was biting her lip and looking rather coyly distressed. I remembered her predicament with the pinned skirt and wondered if I dared ask Angy to make the tea.

110

'Angy! How about brewing the tea?'

'Eh?' His voice was pained and he looked uncompre-hendingly from me to Behag and back to me again.

'Well, you'll either have to brew the tea yourself or go outside while Behag changes her skirt. My hands are thick with flour,' I told him.

Angy got up. 'It's a damty fine thing when a woman has first to change her skirt before she can make the tea,' he remarked sourly as he went outside. Behag slipped into my bedroom and returned her respectable self. Angy, whistling loudly as if to warn us of his reappearance, ambled in and sat down again.

'So you managed to persuade Hector and Erchy to go for the coffin?' I taxed him.

'Ach, there was no persuadin' in it at all,' he replied. 'They were keen enough to go all the time, I could see that.'

I raised my eyebrows. 'They didn't sound in the least keen to me,' I observed.

'Indeed, only the devil himself knows what those two are keen on.' Angy loaded his tea with several spoonfuls of sugar.

'You did!' Behag challenged. Angy responded with a mischievous grin.

'I hope the weather stays calm for them,' I said.

'Indeed I hope so too,' murmured Behag. 'I was hearin' them sayin' the boat was leakin' a good bit since they scraped that rock a week or two back.'

'They'll be safe enough anyway with a coffin aboard,' Angy told her cheerfully.

'What do you mean?' I asked.

'Well, with a coffin aboard supposin' the boat sinks under them they'd still be all right.' He saw my bewilderment. 'Coffins float,' he explained. 'If the boat

111

sinks they'd get into the coffin. It stands to reason for with a couple of oars they'd make land sure enough.'

'It's not an empty coffin,' I reminded him.

Angy shot me a withering glance. 'Aye but two live men's not goin' to drown to save a dead one, are they?' he said reasonably.

As soon as the scones were browned on both sides I wrapped them and a few oatcakes in a teacloth and handed them to Angy. 'You could take some fresh milk for their tea,' I suggested. 'I've plenty and I know fishing boats don't see fresh milk from one week-end to another.' I poured some from the setting bowl into a can. 'Bring me back my cloth and my can,' I called to him as he set off for the shore.

Behag was just being pinned up for the second time when we heard what sounded like the same footsteps again approaching the cottage. Sure enough it was Angy.

'They're sayin' why don't you come aboard an' take a wee strupach with them?' he invited. 'They've just taken their meal an' they're goin' to have a cup of tea and a bite to chase it down.'

'Are you sure?' I asked, pleasantly surprised.

'Aye, that's what they said.'

'I thought they didn't like women on fishing boats,' I demurred. 'Don't women bring bad luck the same as corpses?'

'Not while the boat's moored,' Angy retorted. 'No indeed they're keen enough you should come. See, they don't wish to feel obliged to you for the milk an' the scones. If they had a fry of herrin' aboard now you'd get that instead.'

I understood, and turned to Behag. 'Shall we go?' I asked.

Her expression was eager. 'I believe my cousin's wife's brother is in the crew, is he not?' she asked. 'Him they call "Dodo"?'

'Aye, he's there,' replied Angy. 'At least, the pieces of him are,' he added obscurely.

'I'd love to come,' I admitted. 'I've never been on a real working fishing boat.'

'You'd best hurry then,' instructed Angy. He went outside and Behag again rushed into my bedroom to change.

The skipper and crew hauled Behag and me aboard their boat with awkward gallantry and the cook came up on deck to show us the grey-green loaf which he had taken from its wrapper only that morning. 'Not that the fresh stuff we get is much better,' he complained. 'It's that soft an' doughy you'd think the pollis could use it for takin' fingerprints.' With an expression of disgust he tossed the loaf into the sea.

He invited us into the fo'c'sle where a dusty grey, hot-smelling iron stove was almost covered with kettles and metal teapots. 'Sit you down,' he commanded hospitably and Behag and I inserted ourselves into position on the narrow bench between the bunks and the table. Angy sat beside Behag and the skipper and the two members of the crew took the opposite bench. The cook remained standing, pouring out black tea into permanently tanned mugs and sliding them one at a time along to us.

'I see Hector's boat's away,' observed the skipper in a voice that 'glugged' as if it was being poured out from a bottle.

'Aye, they're takin' that corpse from the mainland,' Angy told him.

'They're takin' it?' The skipper sounded astonished. 'I never thought a Bruach boat would take on a Roman

Catholic corpse,' he remarked, stirring his tea perfunctorily before passing on the spoon to his crew.

'Do they know it's a Roman Catholic?' I asked, thinking of Bruach's rabid presbyterianism and abhorrence of 'Papists'.

Angy nodded.

'So that's why they were so reluctant,' I said.

'Ach, they wouldn't have taken it except for bein' paid double,' replied Angy with a smile.

'Oh, that's terrible,' said Behag, trying hard to disguise her approval for the deal.

'It would be the same if it was the other way round,' said Angy.

I smiled. 'You know,' I told them, 'I've always thought of Bruach people as being some of the most tolerant in the world and yet they have this fearful prejudice against Roman Catholics. I just don't understand it at all.'

'Are you a Papist?' asked Dodo suspiciously.

'No,' I replied, 'but some of my friends are.'

'An' can you trust them?'

'Of course,' I replied, chuckling.

'Aye well,' summed up the skipper. 'It's just the way they have hereabouts. I get on all right myself with them but all the same, there's a somethin'.' He nodded towards one of the lockers. 'Come on, Sammy, with that stuff,' he said.

The cook opened the locker and took out a large tin of pears which he opened.

'You'll take a wee bitty fruit?' he asked me.

At that moment I was not really feeling much like eating anything let alone sweet tinned fruit since the boat was rolling steadily and the fo'c'sle was at the same time both draughty and fuggy. It felt as if someone was packing round my feet with ice cubes while swathing my head in hot towels. However, I smiled acceptance, and the cook carefully slid the tin of pears along the table towards me along with a spoon and a tin of evaporated milk.

'Help yourself,' he invited.

I waited for the expected bowl or plate but to my surprise saw that the cook was opening another large tin of pears which he slid along the table, again with a tin of milk and a spoon, to Behag. Next the skipper was presented with his tins, then the crew and Angy. Finally the cook was able to sit down with his own allotment in front of him. I felt shaken. Seven large tins of pears and seven tins of milk for seven people. The skipper's eye was on me. 'Go on, don't be waitin' for everybody else,' he urged, mistaking my hesitation for politeness. He tipped milk into his tin of pears and began spooning the fruit into his mouth.

'Look, I can't possibly eat all this,' I protested. 'Couldn't I put some out into a dish first to save wasting the rest?' Beside me Behag murmured that she too could never cope with such a quantity.

'Ach, just leave what you don't want,' instructed the skipper, loftily. 'Sammy will get rid of what's left over the side.'

I felt guilty about leaving so many of the pears and more than two-thirds of the tin of milk and would have felt even more guilty had I not observed that only Angy and the cook had managed to dispose of the whole contents of their tins. The skipper and the other two crew had eaten only about half of theirs before pushing the tins away.

The cook picked up a bucket with a rope in its handle. 'Are you sure you can no' eat just a wee bit more?' he enquired, looking solicitously at Behag and me and when we shook our heads he swept all the remaining tins higgledy-piggledy into the bucket and whistling nonchalantly climbed up on to the deck. I had always been brought up on the old adage 'Waste not, want not', and I winced as I heard all that good food splashing into the sea.

The cook came back into the fo'c'sle with the pail rinsed clean. Behag and I exchanged dismayed glances.

'Aye, it's good to have fresh milk for a change,' said the skipper, gulping tea from his mug. 'I fairly enjoy the taste of fresh milk in my tea.' He winked at me, the diffident fisherman's method of saying thank you to a strange woman.

Behag addressed her cousin's wife's brother, Dodo, who was sporting a large piece of sticking plaster behind his right ear, a colourful bruise on his jaw and a deep ruddy scar on the back of one hand.

'Were you in an accident?' she asked him.

'Some accident!' snorted the cook and Dodo's face split into a bashful grin.

'What were you doin'?' pursued Behag.

'I fell down one of these manhole things,' Dodo told her in tones that implied it had been a pleasant experience.

'How did you come to do that?' she pressed anxiously.

'He was drunk,' supplied the skipper. 'Go on, Dodo, tell her the rest of it while you're about it.'

'Ach, right enough we had a good drink on us,' admitted Dodo sheepishly. 'It was on Saturday night when me an' some of my pals were at a dance. We didn't think much of the lassies there so when a gang of strange fellows came in we started tormentin' them. It turned out they were Irish an' it ended up by us bashin' one another about a bit. The next thing we know is somebody's got the pollis so me an' my pals start to run before they can get a hold of us.'

'Only they didn't run fast enough,' interjected the cook.

'Was it run?' echoed Dodo indignantly. 'We ran like tinkers' ponies. "You lead the way, Dodo", my pals shout to me seein' I know this place as well as I know the deck of this boat, so I dodged down this dark entry but by God! hadn't some damty fool left open one of those manhole covers an' plump! down I went into it an' plump! plump!

plump! down came my three pals on top of me. If they'd kept quiet we would have been all right even then but they were swearin' at me so much for takin' them there the pollis heard an' that's how they found us. They carted us off to the station then.'

To me it sounded just like a description of a scene from one of the old 'Keystone Cops' films.

'Did they put you in the cells?' questioned Behag in a horrified voice.

'Aye, until the Monday mornin' an' they charged us five pounds apiece to get out again.' Dodo shook his head regretfully. 'I took ten pounds of good money to go an' enjoy myself on Saturday night an' when I got out of the cells I hadn't a penny in my pocket.'

'But you had five pounds' worth of whisky inside your stomach,' the skipper reminded him.

'Aye,' admitted Dodo. 'You can say it cost me five pounds to get in an' five pounds to get out.'

The skipper drained his cup and pushed it towards the cook for refilling. 'Right enough, the Irish are the ones for fightin',' he opined. 'I believe myself if an Irishman was on a deserted island an' he couldn't find another body to attack he'd have his left hand fightin' his right before he'd be satisfied.'

'When I was in hospital we had an Irish cleaner in the wards,' I recalled with a smile. 'She had rather badly fitting false teeth and one of the patients used to say that even without hearing the cleaner speak she could tell she was Irish because her top set of teeth were always fighting the bottom set.'

'I'll tell you this much,' declared Angy with some ferocity, 'it's not just the humans but even the bloody Irish lobsters fight.'

I could not repress a smile.

'It's true,' reiterated Angy. 'I was workin' on a lobster boat for a time fishin' off the Irish coast so I know what I'm talkin' about.'

'Aye?' said the skipper with a wry smile.

'Well, skipper, you know yourself I've fished lobsters off the coasts of England, Scotland an' Wales in my time an' in the ordinary way when you take the beasts out of the creels an' put them on the deck they'll stay quiet enough till you can tie their claws. But you try doin' that with the Irish lobsters. By God! The minute you put them on the deck the buggers are starin' round with them stalky eyes of theirs an' as soon as one spots another it's straight across the deck they are and tearin' one another to pieces before you can bait a creel. No, if you're fishin' off Ireland you need an extra man to tie the claws of every lobster as it comes out of the creel,' he concluded.

The skipper stood up, glancing at the clock on the bulkhead. I pushed Behag and Behag pushed Angy along the bench.

'We must go back ashore,' we said, and soon we were out on deck.

'I'm right sorry we hadn't a fry to give you,' the skipper apologised. 'But next time we're in maybe.'

'We have plenty of bree,' offered the cook generously. 'D'you care for bree?'

'Bree?' I echoed and shook my head emphatically. Bree is the mixture of blood and salt and fish oil left in the barrel after fresh herring have been salted and kept for about six months. It looks and smells revolting.

'What are you doin' with bree aboard?' asked Angy.

'Ach, we met up with a Norwegian fishing boat last week an' they said would we bring them some bree if we could get a hold of it. We took it for them but we didn't see them so we still have it,' explained the skipper.

'What do they do with it?' I asked.

'Drink it,' replied the skipper and seeing my expression added, 'they nearly come to blows over it they're that keen on it.'

'Great bowls of it they'll drink,' volunteered the cook. 'Honest, they just tilt back their heads, open their mouths an' pour the stuff down their gullets. They'll pay for it if you'll let them.'

Behag and I grimaced at each other.

'They reckon it cures cancer in humans an' foot-an'-mouth in cattle,' said the cook, 'so it must be true there's goodness in it.'

We let ourselves down into the dinghy, the crew dismissing us with enthusiastic promises of a 'good fry' next time they came in.

'Oh, how terrible it was to see all that lovely fruit an' milk goin' over the side,' moaned Behag. 'I felt like jumpin' in after it.'

'That's our skipper,' said Angy proudly. 'Unless there's food to throw over the side he thinks his men aren't bein' well enough fed. He's not a great eater himself, mind, but unless he sees food left on the men's plates he tells the cook to be sure an' provide more next time.'

I had from time to time heard of the prodigality of the catering on some fishing boats: the dictum that there should be 'double helpings for single appetites and all gash straight over the side', but I had never expected to witness it for myself.

'But all those pears!' I expostulated. 'I doubt if we ate more than three tins among the seven of us and yet seven tins were opened. Anyway,' I added, 'surely there was no need to ditch what was left. They would have kept for another meal?'

'It's easy to see you're no' used to boats,' retorted Angy. 'How would you keep opened tins of fruit an' milk an' stuff on a boat that's likely to be jumpin' all over the sea an' over one side then the other when the nets are hauled in?'

'Well,' I began lamely but he cut me short.

'No, it's not "well" at all,' he insisted. 'A man would be comin' down below for a sleep after a heavy night's fishin' an' maybe find tins of milk drippin' into his bunk, or sticky fruit juice all over the fo'c'sle. Indeed, any fisherman findin' that's as likely to throw the cook overboard as the food. No,' he repeated. 'Eat what you want at the time an' dump the rest, that's the only way on a fishin' boat.'

'But,' I persisted, 'if we'd been given plates or bowls we could have taken out only what pears we wanted. There would have been no need to open all seven tins of pears and seven tins of milk.'

'The skipper would have been feared you were stintin' yourselves to be polite,' explained Angy. He backwatered with the oars as we came in close to the shore. 'Anyway,' he added, 'that would have meant there was seven bowls to wash up an' you'd have to have a woman aboard to want to do that.'

Not their Funeral

All day the village had been swathed in mist and silence and fine silky rain that trilled reassuringly from the roof gutter into the half-empty water butts. It had been the sort of day when, since it was impossible to work in the hay, Bruach women felt justified in catching up with their washing or in baking a mountain of scones and oatcakes; a day when Bruach men, anxious to get away from such activity, chose to foregather in the doorway of a neighbour's barn or byre in the hope of being able to pass the time by watching someone else at work. For me it had been a relatively lazy day which, now that evening was thickening the mist, was going, I suspected, to leave me as tired at the end of it as if I had spent it raking and carrying hay. I had finished my evening meal and had put the sewing machine on the cleared table intending to put 'sides to middle' a sheet which had worn thin, but so dim was the light in the kitchen I had to use a magnifying glass to thread the needle. For over two months now I had not needed to light a lamp in the evenings and I felt if I lit one now it would be like betraying what was left of the summer. I decided to leave the sheet-mending for another evening and go to call on Janet at whose house there would undoubtedly be some sort of ceilidh in progress.

'Well, an' here's me thinkin' only this mornin' you were makin' yourself a stranger,' Janet greeted me as I apologised for not having looked in on her for nearly two weeks. 'Come away in, mo ghaoil.' Janet's kitchen was a shade or two darker than my own but like me she had resisted lighting a lamp although on the dresser behind her brother's chair a swaling candle lit a smoked patch on the painted wall and gave him light enough to peer at the previous day's paper. Already in addition to Janet, her brother and myself there were seven other people in the room. Morag was one of them. I had apparently interrupted some story she was telling and punctuating it with a nod to me she continued: 'An' I mind old Ina keepin' them in a drawer till Fergus came home. She showed them to me once. "Fergus keeps on sendin' me these bills or recipits," she grumbled. "An' why should he do that when he's never done it before?" "Ina," says I, "these are neither bills nor recipits. These are five-pound notes." She had more than twenty of them there, just pushed into the drawer of the dresser along with old envelopes an' paper an' bits of string an' postcards. "Five-pound notes?" says she. "I cannot believe those things are worth five pence. Why, there's not a bit of colour on them at all to give them a nice look," she says, starin' at them as if they was no more use than election forms she'd throw at the back of the fire. "That's what they are, Ina," I tell her, but ach, she would not believe me till Fergus came home an' took her up to the Post Office to get a book sayin' it was money he was payin' into it.'

'Ina never did take to readin',' commented old Murdoch. 'I was at school with her an' she was always the dunce, was Ina.'

The door opened and Angy came in, his homespun jacket misted with rain.

'I was just tellin' them about your old aunt Ina,' said Morag, drawing him into the conversation. 'The way she didn't know the recipits Fergus was sendin' were five-pound notes.'

'Aye, I mind hearin' about that,' said Angy, fishing out a damp cigarette. 'I'm thinkin' it's a good thing she never went to Glasgow. The poor old cailleach would have been robbed of everythin' she had.' He went over to the fire and lit his cigarette with a flaming peat. 'Well, Hector an' Erchy are well pleased with the pocketful of five-pound notes they got for doin' their little job,' he announced.

'Are they back?' I asked, and added, 'I didn't see their boat at the mooring.'

'How would you be seein' it in this mist, woman?' Murdoch derided.

'They got back this mornin',' Angy reported. 'An' they would have been back yesterday but for havin' to wait for their money, so they tell me.'

'Did they know who was the corpse?' asked the shepherd.

'Surely they did,' replied Morag and went on to detail the dead man's family tree.

'Aye, aye, I knew the father,' said Murdoch. 'Four sons he had, was it not?'

'Four,' affirmed Morag.

'An' bad luck with all of them, I'm thinkin',' said Murdoch.

'How would that be?' demanded the shepherd.

'Well wasn't the first born deaf an' dumb an' the second died of his lungs an' didn't the third one turn into one of these psychiatrisses?' supplied Murdoch.

'An' now the fourth one has been drowned,' said Morag.

'Drowned, was he?' asked the shepherd and added, 'He'd be drunk likely?'

'No, he was not drunk,' replied Morag. 'They inquested him an' they found no alkali in his body.'

Murdoch rasped disbelief. 'Comin' from that family he was bound to be drunk,' he insisted. 'Why, I never saw the like of it. There was as many bottles of whisky went into that house in a week as come into Bruach in a year.' The old man paused as there came hoots of laughter and muttered accusations of exaggeration. 'Indeed but it's as true as I'm here,' he averred. 'I was workin' on a boat that used to deliver the stuff to them an' I saw it with my own eyes. When the old father of them died I was stuck on the island with the weather while they had his funeral an' I was told by one of the man's own relations that it took thirty-four bottles of whisky to bury him.'

'Thirty-four?' gasped Janet.

'Aye, thirty-four,' repeated Murdoch. 'An' that's a terrible lot of whisky just to put one man in his grave. Mind you,' he added, 'I believe some of the mourners went two or three times to the house to give their condolences as they say, hopin' everybody would be too upset or too drunk to notice them. I heard the widow herself complainin' of that.'

'That was some funeral,' said Angy admiringly.

'What some folks will do for a dram,' said Janet with a sorrowful shake of her head.

'Folks say this one that's been drowned was a queer one when he was home,' said the shepherd. 'I never knew him myself but that's what I've heard folks say.'

'Aye, right enough he was queer,' agreed Morag, who when it came to the inhabitants of the Hebrides was a *Who's Who*. 'I didn't know him either but I knew a woman who lived on the same island. She told me he used to make people gey angry he was that queer in his ways.'

'What sort of things did he do?' I asked.

'Ach well, mo ghaoil, daft things like payin' the income tax when they asked him an' puttin' his clocks backwards and forwards just whenever the government told him to,' she explained.

'That would upset folks right enough,' murmured the shepherd understandingly.

'People reckoned it was him that took the tax mannie to the island,' disclosed Murdoch. 'Seein' one was payin' tax they thought the rest must be cheatin'.'

I was intrigued. 'What happened?' I asked.

'I was there at the time,' he replied. 'An' I saw it for myself.' His eyes glinted. 'Ach, he was only a wee mannie this fellow an' he was that sick on the boat comin' over an' that pale he looked as if he'd been left out in the rain for a long time. He was waitin' on the pier to see the men when they came in from the fishin' an' as soon as the men got word of it they started shoutin' at one another. "There's some tax bugger over there waitin' for us," says one. "Ach, throw him down the fish hold," says another, makin' out they was feelin' right savage, d'you see? Then one of the boats that was unloadin' swung its derrick over an' tipped the whole basketful of fish on top of the poor mannie.' Murdoch wheezed at the memory. 'While he was cleanin' himself up from that they started peltin' him with fish guts. He didn't stay after that but went back to the boat that brought him over. "Take me back to the mainland," he tells the boatman. "There's wild men in this place an' I've suffered enough for the government. If they want taxes from this island they'll need to send the army."' Murdoch probed at the bowl of his pipe with a sharp splinter of wood. 'Right enough, the boatman told us the poor mannie did suffer for he was sick all the way back as well.'

'And did the tax people send anyone else?' I enquired. 'I don't believe they ever did another thing about it except maybe send letters that would go at the back of the fire,' responded Murdoch. 'Ach,' he added, 'the government's plenty of money, why should they give it to the likes of us else?'

'I'm thinkin' the rest of the folks on that island must have been glad when this one that was drowned took himself off to foreign parts to work,' said the shepherd.

'Aye.' Murdoch smiled roguishly. 'I'm thinkin' maybe he would have been drowned a lot sooner in his life if he'd stayed.' He turned to Trina, one of the village girls who had recently completed a teacher-training course. 'You watch the Education don't send you to that island,' he warned her.

'Why, what's wrong with it?' Trina challenged him with a smile.

'You'd have to teach Papists an' Presbyterians together, that's what's wrong with it,' Murdoch told her. 'There's two religions there but only one school.'

'I've never heard that they quarrel about it,' said Trina. 'There was a girl from there at college the same time as myself and she said they were as friendly as folks on any other island.'

'They're friendly enough,' conceded Murdoch, 'except when it comes to the schoolin'. That's when they start their girnin'.'

'Why?' asked Trina.

'D'you not see, lassie,' explained Murdoch patiently, 'they have only one teacher an' the way they've agreed is that if there's more Papist scholars than Presbyterian then the teacher has to be a Papist. If it's the other way round then the teacher has to be a Presbyterian.'

'That sounds fair enough,' said Trina. 'What happens if it's equal numbers?'

'They keep the teacher they have. But if there's one more Papist scholar than Presbyterian then the Papists are pesterin' the education for their own teacher an' the Presbyterians are just as bad if it's the other way round.'

'I'm not surprised the women on that island spend most of their time havin' babies,' observed Angy.

'I believe once there was a teacher there that didn't want to leave the place an' she took a hand in it herself,' Murdoch said.

'It must be a sort of competition,' submitted the shepherd.

'It sounds more like a production drive to me,' said Angy. Throughout the evening the door had been opening and closing as more people entered the room and insinuated themselves into the company. Now Tearlaich burst in, full of confidence and wearing a town raincoat and a trilby hat.

'Were you away!' exclaimed Janet, eyeing his clothes.

'Aye.' Tearlaich returned her glance with mock surprise. 'Did you not know I got a lift from the carrier when he was over with Donny Beag's fencing? I've been to the mainland,' he added.

Except for me probably everyone in the village knew of Tearlaich's journey. What they didn't know was how he had spent his time between then and now.

'Where did you go?' asked Morag, who reasoned that if people did not wish to be asked questions as to their whereabouts or their activities they would take care that nothing they said or did invited them. Tearlaich's attire alone positively cried out for comment.

'I went over to the mainland,' he repeated. 'The carrier was telling me there was to be a big roup on next week so seeing the train was there I got on it an' went to have a look.'

'A roup?' asked Behag with sudden interest.

'Aye, all the furniture and stuff from some old castle,' replied Tearlaich. 'I believe they're going to auction the whole lot of it and the carrier reckons some will go pretty cheap if it's true what he's hearing.'

'Did you get to see any of it?' asked Murdoch.

'Aye, that's why I went.'

'What would you be after wantin' with furniture from a castle?' demanded Morag.

'I'm wantin' a new bed,' returned Tearlaich and smiled at the evident surprise his statement caused.

'The bed you have was good enough for your father,' Murdoch declared. 'Why would it not be good enough for you?'

'It's no' me I'm thinking about,' said Tearlaich. 'But what if I was to take home a wife some day?' He spoke of the possibility of taking home a wife someday as if he might bid for her too at the auction sale. 'I wouldn't want her to sleep in the bed I have,' he resumed. 'She'd be as well sleeping on a dyke.'

'If you took home a wife she wouldn't get much chance to sleep anyway,' Murdoch told him and Tearlaich looked boldly across at Trina who blushed and shook her long hair over her face.

'An' did you see any beds?' enquired Morag.

'Hundreds of them,' answered Tearlaich. 'Honest! You could have slept an army in that castle with the number of beds they had.'

'They possibly did,' I murmured.

'There was one bed though that I couldn't make out at all.' He turned to me. 'Maybe Miss Peckwitt knows more about funny beds than us and she can tell us.'

'Why should I know about funny beds?' I parried.

Tearlaich went on. 'This bed was about seven feet long and about eight feet wide and it had two mattresses on it. One was about five feet wide and the other near enough to three feet. Now why would they have two mattresses on the same bed like that?'

I tried to think of a suitable reason. 'It could be because a single mattress eight foot by seven foot would be difficult to turn regularly,' I hazarded.

'But wouldn't they have the two mattresses the same size then?' suggested Tearlaich.

'That's what I should have thought,' I agreed. 'No, I can't think of a good reason for their being two like that,' I added.

For the first time that evening Janet's brother spoke. 'I've seen one of those beds an' I can tell you the reason for it,' he offered. We looked at him expectantly. 'You mind Dolina across on Rhuna there?' He jerked a thumb towards the seaward wall of the kitchen. 'Now if Mata had a bed like that the three of them would be able to sleep together, the sister in her part of the bed an' Mata an' Dolina in their part. Well, that was the way of it in some of these big castles, only it wasn't the sister that slept with the couple, it was the old mother just so she wouldn't be lonely.'

'Is that true?' asked Janet.

'It's what I was told long ago, that's what they did. You see, they had their separate bedclothes so it wasn't as if they were really sharin' a bed.'

'That was a funny way of doing things,' said Tearlaich. Old Murdoch took out his pipe. 'Indeed they do funnier things than that in some of these old castles,' he stated profoundly and returned his pipe to his mouth.

'Was there anything interesting at the auction?' I asked, turning to Tearlaich.

'Hundreds of things,' he enthused. 'Furniture and rugs and musical instruments and pails and dishes and bowls, indeed every sort of thing you could mention.'

'A piano?' I asked.

'Aye, two of them at least. Why, were you wanting a piano?'

129

I was about to tell him that I very much wanted a piano when the door was slammed back against the wall and Hector and Erchy came in.

'Well, here's the undertakers,' announced Tearlaich.

Erchy ignored him. 'We're wantin' somebody to give us a hand with the dinghy up the shore,' he announced. 'The wireless says it's goin' to blow a gale by mornin'.'

'What wireless?' asked Murdoch indignantly. 'That's not what the wireless at the Post Office said. Force four to five, they said, an' makin' southerly.'

'It doesn't agree with what we've just heard, then,' Erchy told him. 'Force six to gale eight an' veerin' westerly.' He turned to Hector. 'Is that not right, Hector?'

'Aye,' Hector agreed.

'Ach, you cannot expect wirelesses to agree all the time any more than people,' observed Morag soothingly.

Janet's brother got up and going over to the barometer rapped it imperiously. 'The glass is droppin',' he reported.

'Well you don't need to pull your dinghy just yet,' Janet told Erchy. 'Sit you down an' tell us how your trip went.'

'Oh God!' said Erchy and sat down on the floor as if the request had sapped what strength he had left. Hector smiled at the young schoolteacher and she made room for him beside her.

'Knowin' that family I daresay you got a good dram out of it,' said Murdoch.

'Not a dram did we get,' said Erchy. 'Not so much as a look at a bottle of whisky except for what we had with us in the boat.'

'Oh my!' Murdoch was staggered.

'An' the state of that corpse,' grumbled Erchy. 'We needed a barrel of whisky never mind a bottle.' He sighed. 'I'm damty sick of funerals,' he said.

'What happened?' asked Janet curiously.

'Well, we got to the pier,' began Erchy, 'an' there was the coffin ready for loadin' but when we went to get it aboard we was near sick with the smell of him. He'd been coffined in one of these foreign places an' they hadn't done it properly so he'd gone rotten. The men on the pier agreed with us that nobody was goin' to carry it aboard like a coffin should be by rights. "Get the derrick," they told us. So we went to see the man with the crane an' asked him would he load it on board for us. "I'm not supposed to lift coffins with the crane," he says. "Coffins are supposed to be treated with respect." "Well, we're no' carryin' him," says I. "He's too rotten." Anyway, the crane fastens on to him an' hoists up the coffin an' one of the pier men shouts to the crane driver, "Hey, Ronny, don't tilt him now or he'll spill out."'

'Oh here!' murmured Janet with a shudder.

'That's what they said. An' we had to put the bloody coffin on the stern so that the smell would blow away from us. Ach, it was terrible!' He gave a snort of disgust.

'An' did none of the man's friends come along with the coffin?' asked Morag.

'Aye, three of them,' replied Erchy. 'But they had a good drink on them before they came aboard an' they just lay down an' slept all the way.'

'An' what happened when you got to the island?' pursued Janet. 'Did you have to carry the coffin then?'

'We did not,' said Erchy. 'Ach, there was seven or eight folks waitin' there an' with the three we had there was plenty.'

'Was there no priest?'

'Aye, he was down too, fussin' around like a hen on a hot girdle, an' before they'd lift the coffin off the boat he took them all up to the chapel with him. They was there about half an hour an' they all came back wipin' their mouths an' smellin' of whisky.'

131

'An' you didn't get a dram yourselves?' interrupted Murdoch.

'None but the smell of theirs,' reiterated Erchy. 'Maybe if we'd followed them up to their chapel we would have got one but there's some things you can't do even for whisky.' He looked around the company, confident of their approbation.

' "Men meet but the hills do not",' quoted Murdoch. 'So they unloaded the coffin themselves,' prompted Janet.

'They did so. An' there was the priest wavin' his hands an' tellin' them, "Be careful boys, now," and "Gently, boys," an' them afraid would they jolt it an' have the priest swearin' at them for bein' careless.' He looked across at Hector. 'Was that not the way of it?' he asked.

Hector looked up and smiled wide-eyed confirmation. 'Indeed it was so,' he said. 'Tsey took tsat much care carryin' it ashore you'd think it was a case of whisky tsey was handlin', not a coffin.'

'Angy was sayin' you had to stay the night before you could get your money,' Morag said.

'Aye.'

'That was no' right,' said Morag. 'When a job has been done a man shouldn't have to wait to be paid for it.'

'Why was that?' asked Tearlaich. 'They'd agreed to pay what you'd asked, hadn't they?'

'They had, but when it came to actually handin' over the money they started sayin' it was too much.'

'Ach!' sneered Murdoch. 'Gettin' money out of them Papists is like gettin' butter out of a dog's throat.'

'But you got it in the end?' enquired Angy.

'We got it. An' we told them they was lucky we didn't charge them extra for the smell.'

There came a sudden puff of smoke down the chimney. Erchy stood up. 'We'd best away an' pull that dinghy,' he said. 'That's the wind on its way already.' He went out, followed by all the younger men.

'I must go too,' I told Janet. Behag followed me to the door and we stepped out into a moonlit night with no trace of mist.

'I would like fine to go to the roup,' she confided wistfully.

'Why not go then?' I asked, avoiding her glance.

'Would you be thinkin' of goin' yourself?' she enquired diffidently. 'I hate travellin' on my own.'

When Tearlaich had mentioned the pianos at the sale the idea of going to the auction had indeed crossed my mind but it was immediately followed by the thought of haymaking, the arrangements I should have to make before I could leave my cow and poultry and by a mental review of the difficulty of getting a piano over to Bruach and eventually into my cottage. Much as I yearned for a piano I had let the idea slip away into the limbo of all the other ideas I had at times become enraptured with, but Behag's remark made me think again. Perhaps I could arrange to get to the roup and perhaps I could even bring a piano back with me. 'I'll let you know tomorrow,' I told her as we said good night.

The sky was clear, wiped clean by wind, and I walked thoughtfully homewards, almost hearing the notes of a Chopin nocturne and aware that my fingers ached to run over the keys of a piano. On reaching my cottage I stood looking up at the full moon tossed in the branches of the rowan tree and the evening star blinking over the hills, and worked out how long I could spare away from the croft and who would look after Bonny and the hens whilst I was away. Morag would, I was certain, but with Behag away also would it be too much for her to cope with? I went to bed and slept on my project. No doubt it would sort itself out by the morning.

Going to the Roup

By morning the forecast gale was strafing the village, flattening the uncut grass, tearing at the windows and bombarding the hay already cocked and rough-tied with grass ropes. As soon as I woke I rushed outside to inspect the damage to my own cocks and was agreeably surprised to find that only three out of the nine I had so industriously stooked and tied two days earlier had been ravaged by the wind. I blessed the mist and rain of the previous day which had dampened down the outside of the cocks so that they had settled into snug igloo shapes, trimmed to resist the assault of the gale. As I gathered up the hay which the wind had peeled off and slid into the lee of the damaged cocks I had cause to be grateful once again to Morag for her instructions on how to weave the traditional hay ropes which undoubtedly had been responsible for saving much of my hay. The hay rope was a simple but effective device for securing cocks and it was achieved by gathering strands of grass from the top on the windward side of the cock, twisting them and at the same time drawing in more hay as you worked downwards until with a final twist you tucked the rope in firmly under the base of the cock, being careful that you did not let the wind in so that the whole thing blew away. Then you did the same on the lee side. I repaired the three cocks, tucked in the ropes on the other six more firmly and started back towards the cottage. The sea was swirling white, the horizon a jumble of watery peaks, but although the crofts were being lashed by sea spray there was no rain. I recited to myself the weather lore I had learned in rhyme:

'If the wind before the rain,
Hoist your topsails up again',

which, so the old sailors explained, meant that it would probably be a short blow with the rain coming in later to quell the wind. On the other hand:

'If the rain before the wind,
Your topsail halyards you must mind',

which again being interpreted meant the wind would be strong enough to drive away any threatened rain. In other words, it foretold a long, strong blow. I looked up at the thick grey clouds racing across the sky, unsure whether or not I hoped they would soon burst. If they did it would probably result in there being constant rain for the next few days which would not improve the hay but if they did not and the wind continued unabated I doubted if my cocks would withstand its onslaught. Hay making was always a worry and because of the malicious weather and the dishevelled terrain it was a worry that lasted a long time. Though cutting might be commenced at the end of July even in a good season it was likely to be well into October before the hay was finally stacked for the winter. I debated whether to take proper ropes and stones to tie and weight down the cocks but if I did that and the rain came the weighted ropes would make neat channels in the hay which would direct the rain deep into the cock, sending it mouldy and rotten. Back at my cottage, I stood in front of my barometer. It had dropped but not dramatically and when I tapped it the needle stayed steady. I decided to do nothing more about my hay until I had talked to some of my neighbours and listened to their predictions.

The rain came when I was out on the moor looking for Bonny. While I milked her the rain dribbled from her flanks and from the sleeves of my oilskin into the pail so that the milk took on a muddy-greyish look. I smiled to myself, recalling how horrified I would have been in my pre-Bruach days had I been expected to drink milk produced under such conditions. Now I knew that dribble from cows' flanks, oilskins and even from less salutary sources made no noticeable difference to the flavour of the milk and so far as hygiene was concerned I preferred fresh Highland germs to those that could be expected in the vicinity of a town or factory dairy. I gave Bonny the remainder of her potach, thanked her and sent her away with a gesture – she was too wet to pat – and turned into the wind and rain, making for home. Even with the lid tightly clamped down the milk splashed out as the wind buffeted the pail, lifting it and at times almost wresting it from my grasp; the rain was drumming on my sou'wester, streaming down my oilskin and running into my boots. It was stinging my face and filling my eyes so that I was constantly blinking to see where I was going and when, after taking advantage of the shelter offered by a narrow strath between two outcrops of rock, I came out again into the teeth of the storm the wind spun me round, whisking away my breath and making me feel like a chattel of the storm, seeing nothing but rain; no sea, no sky, with only occasional glimpses of the moors to help me find my way home.

After lunch I started to make bread and teacakes and the kitchen was full of the yeasty, floury smell of bread baking when the door banged open to admit Morag. She pushed the door closed with a practised shoulder and let down the latch.

'My, but it's a coarse wind you catch here,' she informed me as she slid out of the top layer of coats she was wearing. 'I thought my own house was the bad one for the wind but I'm thinkin' your own is worse.'

'It depends on the direction,' I reminded her. 'Yours gets the north-easterly pretty badly but this one is the wind I'm most exposed to. It has one advantage, though.' I nodded at the wire tray where the bread was cooling. 'My oven is always much hotter when the wind is from this direction.'

'Aye, an' you make good use of it, mo ghaoil. Indeed, there's nobody like the English for bakin' in an oven,' she told me.

I split and buttered some teacakes and we ate them while they were warm and doughy and swimming in butter. Morag was just helping herself to her third piece when the door opened again but with more violence this time and Erchy came in.

'I was just down seein' if there was anythin' worth while comin' ashore,' he announced in reply to our enquiring looks. 'We got a letter a night or two ago from my cousin that's workin' on a timber boat. He reckoned they'd be passin' through the channel out there yesterday an' he always tries to throw some good planks over the side thinkin' they might wash ashore here.'

Bruach had its share of beachcombers, ranging from the regulars who went daily to search for anything that might conceivably be of use, to the dilettantes like myself who went only when the weather was fine enough, but during gales when the men of the village could find little else to do they rushed down to appropriate for themselves stretches of shore, just as fishermen select stretches of a river, and there they crouched in the indifferent protection of a boulder, straining to be the first to spot any loot the sea might bring in. The most dedicated – some said the greediest – stayed out all night, the rest stayed for perhaps four or five hours before they gave in and returned to their own or someone else's home where they could be sure of a hot drink and a bite to eat.

'An' did you get anythin' for your trouble?' asked Morag.

'Only a couple of trawl bobbins an' a few fish boxes,' confessed Erchy. 'But there's time enough. Maybe I'll get down in the mornin' at first light an' get a hold of somethin' good.'

'You didn't by any chance get any of those glass net floats?' I asked. I was collecting the coloured glass floats to edge a border in my flower garden.

'Aye, I got two,' Erchy replied. 'They're outside.' He eyed the teacakes. 'You'll get them for a couple of those scones you have there.'

I laughed and started to split and butter more teacakes.

'Eating them hot like this is probably going to give you terrible indigestion,' I warned. 'But I don't suppose that will put you off, will it?'

He winked. 'Indeed I wouldn't be put off supposin' you told me they'd give me the terrible plague,' he assured me and clamping the two halves together he disposed of the first teacake in two bites. I continued splitting and buttering.

'I hear you're away to the roup next week,' he observed, halfway through his second teacake.

'Am I?' I asked.

'Behag's expectin' you to go,' put in Morag. 'She's after makin' all her plans.'

'I didn't say I'd go,' I repudiated and chided myself for having forgotten that in Bruach anything less than an emphatic refusal was taken as acquiescence. 'I don't know if I can get away,' I went on. 'I've still to find someone to see to Bonny and the hens and with the day being so wild and wet I haven't got round to asking anyone yet.'

'An' do you need to ask?' Morag reproached me. 'Can I no' see to your cow for you the same as I have many a time before now.'

'But Behag will be away too,' I reminded her. 'Otherwise I should have come straight to you.'

'An' when would Behag be any use milkin' a cow?' she demanded scornfully.

'I was just thinking of all the extra work for you,' I pointed out.

'But isn't my cousin comin' tomorrow on the bus to stay with me from Glasgow,' she told me.

'Which one's that?' asked Erchy.

'The one that was in hospital a while back,' replied Morag.

'Is she better, then?'

'She's better,' acknowledged Morag. 'Though I believe they were still givin' her egyptians for the pain for a week or two after she came out.'

'Well, she's not going to be of any help to you, is she?' I argued. 'Surely having a convalescent on your hands is going to make even more work for you?'

'Not at all,' denied Morag. 'She can see to the boilin' of the potatoes an' she can feed the hens an' she'll be glad to do it.'

'But if she's not well,' I began.

'Indeed there's nothin' wrong with her at all,' refuted Morag, who, possibly because of her experience with Hector, was disinclined to believe reports of ill health from any other of her relatives. 'Nothin' that a month or two in Bruach won't cure.' She put down her empty cup. 'I'll milk your cow for you an' willingly,' she repeated. 'An' seein' my own cow's startin' to go dry I'll be well pleased to get the extra milk for a whiley.'

I thanked her and pointed out that I still had to get someone to come and feed my poultry. Even had Morag offered I could not have allowed her to take on this extra task. The milking was not so demanding since she would be going out to the moors to milk her own cow but feeding the hens would entail her coming down to my croft in the early morning and again in the evening.

Erchy said: 'I'd feed your hens for you if I'm about but if the weather clears I'll be at the lobsters the best part of the day.' He looked slightly distressed. 'I couldn't promise,' he added.

'If the weather clears I ought not to be away from home anyway,' I told him. 'Not with all that hay out in cocks.'

'They're sayin' this rain's on for a week or more,' asserted Morag. 'They're expectin' the wind to drop shortly but without the wind they say there'll be nothin' but rain an' mist an' rain again till the moon changes an' that's ten days away yet.'

'They' were the elders of the village. The pipe-smoking, pontificating old men whose weather predictions were at least as reliable as more official ones.

'That's some consolation, anyway,' I said. 'I shan't feel too guilty about the hay.'

'There's no need to feel guilty about anythin',' comforted Morag. 'Sheena was sayin' she'd be pleased enough to come an' feed your hens for you if she'd get the eggs. She has her brother an' his family with her an' she's girnin' that they swallow eggs as fast as gulls swallow fish guts.'

'That's splendid!' I said. 'My hens are laying well just now so I shan't be ashamed to go and ask her.'

'I don't believe there's any need to ask her,' Morag informed me. 'I believe she's made up her mind to it already.' She got up and started to put on her coat. 'Will I tell Behag you'll be goin', then?' she asked, adding in a lower voice, 'If the Lord spares you.'

'Yes,' I replied. 'I'll be going.'

As soon as word got around that Behag and I were going to drive in my car to the roup first Tearlaich and then Angy announced they would be bestowing their company on us.

'There won't be much room,' I told them. 'And it's a long drive.'

'Ach, we'd sooner be uncomfortable than lonely,' they replied and so it was arranged we should all cram into 'Joanna' and leave first thing on the following Tuesday morning.

As the old men had forecast the rain had continued and though the wind had dropped it was still harrying the sea enough to throw clouds of spray over the ferry as we crossed to the mainland. It poured over the car roof and coursed down the windscreen.

'If we'd gone by train, now, we wouldn't have the car to give us shelter,' Behag commented, indicating the two or three foot passengers who were seeking shelter behind the car.

'Poor things,' I said. 'I hope they're not going on the train. If they are they'll stay wet until lunchtime at least.'

'Ach, they won't mind,' retorted Tearlaich. 'On this ferry they don't take your fare if you get wet.'

We bounced off the ferry, up the mainland slip and drove for a couple of hours without seeing another moving thing. Occasionally we glimpsed a burn in spate tumbling and foaming under the bridge over which we were driving; occasionally there was a straggle of stunted trees, occasionally a dwelling of some sort but most of the time the rain enclosed us, taxing the efficiency of the windscreen wipers. The car grew so stuffy that Behag had continually to wipe the windscreen clear of mist.

'Anyone know where we might get a bite to eat?' I asked.

Tearlaich responded immediately. 'I know a hotel not far from here. I used to know one of the waitresses.' There could hardly have been a hotel in the whole of the Highlands where Tearlaich did not claim to know one of the waitresses, and admittedly his knowledge appeared to serve him well. He frequently told tales of how he had got himself stranded at various times, 'and if it hadn't been for this waitress I knew I would have had to spend the night out on the hill and without a bite to eat'.

'It's a wonder these waitresses don't get into trouble sometimes the way they look after you,' observed Behag and added hurriedly, 'I mean, from their bosses.'

'Ach, I'm always away before the bosses appear in the morning,' replied Tearlaich. 'Except for once when I had to sleep under the table in the kitchen.'

'How was that?' asked Angy.

'This hotel had gone kind of swanky and they'd got in one of these foreigners to manage it. Well, he comes down in the night to get something from the kitchen an' he finds me there…'

'By yourself?' interrupted Angy incredulously.

'I was by that time,' acknowledged Tearlaich with a wink. 'Anyway,' he continued, 'in this fellow comes. "You get out!" he orders, only his language was a lot worse than that and when I didn't offer to get out he started screaming at me: "Bugger off, you." "Take it easy," I told him. "I'm doin' nobody any harm here and I'll be away at first light." But no, he wasn't going to have me stay and he went off out of the kitchen swearin' to bring down the owner to turn me out. Well, I knew the owner had no reason to like me seeing he was a Campbell and me a MacDonald so I got out.' He chortled. 'All the same, I got my own back on that foreigner fellow, I can tell you.'

'How?' I asked.

'Well, d'you see there was this big pan of porridge at the side of the stove all ready for warming up for the guests' breakfasts and the other side of the stove there was a big baking dish full of raw eggs all taken from their shells and set ready to go straight into the oven. I lifted the tray of eggs and tipped half of them into the pan of porridge and stirred it all up so that it looked OK. Then I buggered off like I was told to.'

'It must have been damty queer porridge they got for their breakfasts,' said Angy.

'Did you ever hear what happened?' Behag asked.

'No, I never did. Ach, I knew fine I'd best not go back that way again for a while so I didn't think about the waitress any more.'

'Whereabouts was this hotel?' I enquired.

'Well, now,' said Tearlaich, 'it'll be only just about a mile along the road now. Like I was sayin', I know this waitress so if she's still there she'll see we get a good meal.'

'Tearlaich!' I exclaimed. 'Do you mean you're taking us to the hotel where you spoiled the porridge?' In the mirror I saw his uncontrite expression. 'Oh, no,' I told him. 'I'm not going there in your company.'

'Ach, it's all right now,' he soothed. 'I know for a fact the foreigner's been gone over a year so I don't need to bother any more.'

'Isn't there anywhere else we can get a meal?' I pleaded.

'Not that I know of,' returned Tearlaich. 'Not for another ten miles anyway.' He rustled a paper bag. 'Here, take a mint,' he invited. 'It'll stop you getting indigestion.'

'Tearlaich's a right joker,' enthused Angy when everyone was steadily sucking.

'Indeed if it's jokers we're speaking of then there's the biggest one of them sitting right beside me at this minute,' retaliated Tearlaich.

'Angy?' asked Behag.

'Aye. Why only the week before he came back to Bruach didn't he and his pals kidnap a bride and groom the night before they was to get married.'

'That's not so unusual,' I reminded Tearlaich. I had heard of bawdy escapades sometimes taking place the night before a wedding though I had never been aware of such a happening in Bruach.

'No, but this was one of the best,' Tearlaich continued fervently. 'They got a hold of this lorry and an old lavatory from the builder's yard and they stuck this lavatory on the lorry and tied the bride sitting down on it with a po on her head. Then they drove round and round the place till folks was near sick with laughing.'

'Oh, my,' commented Behag.

'We got the groom, too, don't forget,' Angy reminded him.

'Aye, so they did and seeing they was friendly with one or two of the night nurses up at the hospital they carted him up there, tied him down on the table and gave him an enema.'

'Really!' I was horrified.

'Honest to God, they did,' averred Tearlaich. He turned to Angy. 'I believe the groom wasn't too pleased about it, was he?'

'I should think not,' I told him.

'Aye, well it wasn't so much what we did to him he minded but he was wearin' his weddin' trousers when we got a hold of him an' they got a bit torn.' Angy explained. 'He said we was to get him a new pair but ach! where would we get new trousers till the tinkers come round?'

'You certainly carry your jokes to the limit,' I remarked.

'The limit indeed,' confirmed Tearlaich. 'He's lucky he hasn't been banned from one or two of the pubs on the mainland for some of the tricks he's got up to.'

'Such as…' I encouraged.

144

'Such as,' he began, winding down his window to throw out a cigarette butt. A small wedge of coolness probed down the back of my neck before the window was closed again tightly. 'By God! There's still some rain out there,' he observed superfluously.

'You were going to tell us about another of Angy's tricks,' I reminded him.

'Aye, well there was the moocher, wasn't there, Angy?'

'Oh, him,' muttered Angy with a show of reticence. 'He deserved all he got.'

'What happened to him?' I enquired.

'D'you know what a "moocher" is, for a start?' asked Tearlaich.

'I've always taken it to be a lazy, good-for-nothing sort of fellow,' I answered.

'No, well to us a "moocher" is one of them fellows that if you leave your drink for a minute in the pub he nips in while your back's turned and drains the glass. That's right, isn't it, Angy?'

Angy's smiling face was reflected in the driving mirror. 'So Angy decides to teach him a lesson,' resumed Tearlaich. 'And he goes to the chemist's and buys a box of worm pills.'

'For dogs,' interrupted Angy.

'Aye, for dogs,' agreed Tearlaich. 'Now go on,' he urged Angy. 'Tell her yourself what you did.'

Angy took up the story. 'The instructions on the box said one pill for small dogs, two for medium and three for large dogs.' He smiled. 'Well, I reckoned the moocher was twice as big as a large dog so the next time he was in the pub before I left my pint of beer I slipped six of the pills into it. Sure enough when I got back my glass was empty and the moocher was gone.'

'Oh, here,' remonstrated Behag. 'It's a wonder you didn't poison the man.'

'Poison, hell!' scoffed Angy. 'No, but he was off work for three weeks afterwards with what the doctor said was a bad dose of dysentery,' he added with deep satisfaction.

'Here's the hotel,' proclaimed Tearlaich as a long low building loomed up out of the rain. I pulled 'Joanna' off the road and we went inside. Like most Highland hotels it was clean and cold and a little intimidating. Tearlaich disappeared muttering something about arranging for food and Angy led us unerringly to a small bar where he first rapped, then thumped and eventually yelled for service. His summons brought a tartan-kilted, sporraned and tweed-jacketed man who gave us a greeting that was as cheerless as the day itself and served us our drinks with an air that conveyed that bar service was not his normal occupation and that we were not the class of customer the hotel normally catered for. Once we had our drinks he disappeared again.

'He's a snooty one,' I commented.

'Snooty?' echoed Angy. 'No, it's not that what's wrong with him. It's just he hasn't learned yet how to behave right. He's learned himself to dress like a toff but it'll take him a long time to learn the rest, for when I first knew him his head was that empty his cap used to rattle when he talked.'

'I was thinkin' I'd seen him before,' said Behag.

'An' so you have,' Angy assured her. 'The last time I saw that man he had a broken-down old fish van takin' seconds kippers round the villages. He wasn't wearin' any of his fancy clothes then, he couldn't afford them, an' his hands was that black with engine grease he left thumbprints on every kipper like they say St Peter left on the haddocks.'

Tearlaich came back looking mightily pleased with himself. 'They say we can take our soup right away if we've a mind,' he informed us.

146

'I've a mind,' I replied.

'An' so have I,' said Angy, tossing down the last of his drink. 'Lead the way, boy,' he instructed and we followed Tearlaich through to the dining room of which we were the sole occupants.

'Did you see your waitress?' asked Behag as we took our seats.

'Aye, I did. But she's cook now, that's why we're gettin' such big helpings.' Tearlaich regarded with approbation the four deep plates of steaming Scotch broth that were being put before us by a young waitress.

'And did she mention the incident of the porridge?' I probed.

'Only that she didn't hear of any complaints about it,' returned Tearlaich lightly as he tied his table napkin round his neck. 'You'll be seeing her yourself in a whiley. She says she's coming to drink a cup of tea with us when we've finished eating.'

'Is she still keen on you, then?' asked Angy.

'Aye, I believe she is,' replied Tearlaich modestly.

As soon as the young waitress had cleared the table the cook appeared with a large tray of tea and biscuits. Greeting us with great cordiality she sat down and Tearlaich made the introductions.

'Angy,' she repeated when she heard his name. 'Now would it be your father that had the half of the boat with my own Uncle Seamus at one time? Him that had the wooden leg?'

'I believe you're right,' agreed Angy. 'I mind my father speakin' of workin' with somebody that had a wooden leg.'

'I could see the likeness,' the cook complimented herself smugly. 'An', Behag,' she went on, 'Tearlaich was sayin' you married Hector that was Morag McDugan's sister's boy?'

Behag smiled and nodded confirmation.

'An' they were sisters to deaf Ruari, were they not? Him that was workin' for a time over on the mainland along with that fellow that was always threatenin' to commit suicide by stranglin' himself with his own hands an' then only died of the measles.'

The trace of mockery in the cook's voice kindled brief smiles from the two men but appeared to disconcert the gentle Behag who stared mournfully down at her tea. I was accustomed now to the knowledge that wherever Bruachites went they invariably discovered family connections that had to be enthusiastically researched and confirmed and as always I soon began to feel excluded. My attention wandered to the innumerable stags' heads that made a melancholy frieze around the room; the stuffed wild cat and the various fish in their glass cases. When the second pot of tea had been disposed of I made a move to go and after some hesitation and a good deal of whispering and chaffing between Tearlaich and the cook we were back again in 'Joanna' with the rain still falling relentlessly.

At the hotel where Behag and I had booked for the night we parted company with Angy and Tearlaich. They, again on the principle that they would sooner be uncomfortable than lonely, proposed to call on a relative of Angy's who, they felt sure, would insist on offering them a shakedown for the night.

'See you at the roup,' they called.

'See you at the roup,' we replied, though with such a selection of pubs to visit I doubted if either of them would recollect the ostensible purpose of their trip. 'And if you're not here by three o'clock tomorrow we go without you,' I threatened.

'I believe the bitch would, too,' I overheard Angy murmur to Tearlaich.

'What shall we do with ourselves tonight?' I enquired of Behag. 'The shops are closed but we could go to the pictures.'

'Would you mind if we took a look round the shop windows first,' Behag asked. 'It seems so long since I could look at things that weren't just drawings in a catalogue.'

'Of course,' I told her, and was glad she had suggested it.

To dawdle round town streets in the pouring rain looking in the windows of closed shops does not seem such a crazy thing to do when like Behag and me your eyes have for years lit on no more an enticing display of merchandise than the confusion of biscuits, homespun socks, pot-menders and boiled sweets in the grocer's window or the welter of garments in the bundles carried by the tinkers. It was more than three years since either of us had seen a real shop and we were perfectly happy, in our town wear of brogues, burberries and sou'westers, touring the quiet, dripping streets. When Behag declared she was satisfied we had a meal in the cinema restaurant before taking our seats in the auditorium.

'How long is it since you was at the fillums?' asked Behag.

'Oh, seven years at least,' I replied after a moment's thought.

'It's ten or more since I was there,' said Behag. 'I'm lookin' forward to it more than I can say.'

'I believe I am too,' I confessed.

We settled ourselves in our seats with a box of chocolates I had bought to celebrate the occasion and as the lights dimmed I remembered the excitement that moment always used to bring. But then the music started. Behag and I turned to each other aghast at the volume of the noise. We put our hands over our ears until the cartoons came on and the music was suppressed by other sound effects. The big film began. I believe it had what is generally described as a star-studded cast but I found every one of them lifeless and tedious. After the lilting Gaelic voices I had grown so used to they appeared to speak without inflexion and almost without moving their lips. The significant pauses while one character looked deep into another's eyes were so dragged out that I found myself tapping my foot with impatience. I looked at Behag to note her reaction and saw she was fast asleep. After enduring for another half-hour I was cramped and hot and utterly bored and Behag still slept soundly. I prodded her.

'Let's go,' I suggested. 'You're obviously tired and I'm bored and this blessed thing is going to continue for a couple of hours yet.'

She made no objection. 'I saw what happened in the beginning,' she confided as we were walking back to the hotel. 'But I wonder what happens at the end?'

'I don't know or care,' I replied. 'But I do know if I'd had to sit there much longer and watch close-ups of sweaty faces it would have spoiled my appetite for these chocolates and I'm damned if I'm going to let that happen.'

Back in the hotel she said, 'It's funny, I used to like the fillums but now I seem as if can't take to them at all.' She yawned. 'I think that's what sent me to sleep, it all bein' so slow.'

'Slow!' I exclaimed. 'Why, they even sweated in slow motion.' I proffered the box of chocolates. 'I'm always hearing that life is lived at a much faster pace nowadays than it was even ten years ago but from what I've seen tonight I'd say the film producers haven't noticed it.'

In bed with the light out I lay and listened to the noises of the town and thought of life in Bruach and how slow that always seemed and I realised suddenly how quick and how constantly alert one's mind had to be compared with people in town. Admittedly in town one had to keep a good look-out to avoid traffic or bumping into other people but at least that look-out was, or should be, reciprocal. In Bruach the sole responsibility for evading hazards was on oneself and no one else. We had to watch where we walked in case a foot went into a rabbit hole or a bog; we had to spot which clumps of heather would brush out of one's path and which would tangle one's foot and cause a fall; we noted cracks in hill paths that could easily become minor landslides; we watched the sky for signs of weather and the tides if we were going out in a boat, and all the time we had to look out to see which way the cattle were working in their search for grass so that we should not waste time when we went to milk or feed them; to watch them for signs of bloat or mastitis and sheep for signs of maggot or footrot or any of the many other ills which afflict them. We noted any gathering of crows which might indicate a carcase or at best a sick animal to be rescued; we plotted the source of smoke in case it was an incipient heather fire, and we kept an eye alert for moor gates left open, fences collapsed, tilting hay or peat stacks; stones among the grass that would blunt the scythe; the tracks of a rat near a potato store; a hen laying away from the nest; a loose stone in a dyke which if not firmly wedged in again could bring down a whole section of the dyke with the next storm or with the rubbing of an animal.

'Ahhhhhh.' From Behag's bed there came a long musical yawn. 'I'd like fine to know what happened in the end,' she murmured sleepily.

151

Pianissimo

The hall where the roup was to be held was more full of people than furniture when Behag and I arrived and as we wandered deviously among the damp onlookers we watched prospective buyers bouncing on beds and settling into chairs like visitors at a ceilidh. I caught the sound of a piano and made my way in the direction from which it came, leaving Behag to admire a bundle of rugs which she was already coveting. A youth was prodding at the jaundiced keys of an old upright piano and I waited for him to tire of his play before I ventured with similar inexpertise to try them for myself. The notes sounded muffled with damp, several were completely dumb but when I wanted to inspect the inside I found I was prevented from doing so by two arthritic old men who had each appropriated an end of the piano and braced himself against it, with folded arms resting determinedly on the lid. I suspected the shock of being asked to move might prove too much for them and I remained standing nearby hoping they would detach themselves before the auctioneer got round to selling it. It appeared that the old men were not remotely interested in the sale.

'Did you try the liniment I gave you for your rheumatics?' one was enquiring of the other.

'Aye, I tried it.'

'Did you rub it on or did you put some in a basin of water an' soak your feet in it like I told you?'

'I did neither.' The voice sounded a little startled. 'I swallowed it.'

'Oh God!' The ejaculation was followed by a brief lull in the conversation and then the questioner began again. 'An' did even that not help your rheumatics at all?'

'It did not. Indeed there's nothin' helps my rheumatics save a good prayer of damnin' every mornin'.' The morose reply was followed by a duet of wheezy chuckles.

As Tearlaich had reported there were at least two pianos in the sale. I went on searching for others but finding only one, which was a grand and therefore out of the question, I returned to my position near the upright. The old men were still *in situ* but now two women were trying simultaneously to pick out the tune of 'Kathleen Mavourneen' while an attendant male alternately nodded and belched approval.

'Oh God! Bridie!' declared one of the women in indisputably Irish accents. 'I can feel tears comin' with the sound of it.' She touched her eyes with the tips of her fingers.

'Sure, Teresa, aren't I the same myself?' responded the other fervently and in an even stronger brogue. 'I declare the last time I heard it played was in a pub an' I had to rush off to the lavatory I was that affected.'

'With the tears,' suggested Teresa.

'Just that. Rainin' down they were.'

'Ah, you'd be that touched,' sympathised Teresa while Bridie nodded and murmured something about her 'lovely land' and the attendant male belched consolingly.

At that moment the auctioneer appeared and made his way to the desk and after giving us a brief résumé of how he intended to conduct the sale the bidding began for the larger items of furniture. At this juncture I was only mildly

153

interested in the goods being auctioned but I was thoroughly intrigued by the conversation of the old men which continued despite the penetrating voice of the auctioneer, the hammering and the constantly murmured comments.

'Ach, he was a decent kind of man for all that, with a strong look of a minister about him when he was dressed,' one of the old men told his companion.

'An' did they not get the doctor then?'

'They asked him but he didn't come except to help dig the grave.'

This piece of information was followed by some mumbled comments which I could not catch but then the first old man was speaking again. 'He never left no will. He was a man that enjoyed seein' his relatives quarrel when he was alive an' I daresay he wouldn't want to give up his enjoyment when he was dead.'

'Then the lawyers will get the most of it,' concluded the second old man.

The auctioneer's men approached and I realised the piano was about to go up for sale. Mentally I had set a price over which I must not go but when the time came I continued bidding until I had exceeded it by two pounds and the piano became mine. Admittedly I need only have gone thirty shillings above my limit but at the crucial moment the Irish male behind me belched and the auctioneer went up ten shillings. The old men gave me congratulatory nods but still clung to it and I was glad that it would be the carrier and not myself who would have the job of prising it away from them.

Some of the smaller items were now coming up for sale and I bought a set of copper bottles because I liked their shape and an old copper warming pan which I suspected would have to be useful as well as ornamental. Behind me the two Irish women were commenting on how cheap the last jumble of items in the sale were going. A lot comprising a step-ladder, a zinc bath and a sweeping brush was displayed. The auctioneer managed to push the bidding up from one shilling which was the minimum bid he would accept to two shillings.

'Come on,' he urged, 'we don't intend to give things away.' There came a bid of another sixpence and he knocked them down for that amount.

'Mother of God for half a crown!' gasped one of the Irish women, and a few moments later when three bedroom chairs went for the minimum bid there was an ejaculated 'Jesus Christ for a shilling!' In fact the Jesus Christ bid had been my own and I glanced behind me half smiling at the two women. 'You can't lose anything on that,' one of them assured me.

'Well, did you get your piano?' Tearlaich, Angy and Behag had threaded their way through the crowd to my side. The men's breath was swamped with whisky fumes and their eyes were over bright but they showed no other signs of inebriation.

'I did,' I replied. 'And several other things besides. Did you get your bed, Tearlaich?' He nodded affirmation.

'I got this rug.' Behag unrolled the bundled rug she was carrying. 'Will it go in the car to get home, d'you think?' I doubted it.

'I got a mangle,' said Angy.

'A mangle?' echoed Behag in surprise. 'Why would you be wantin' a mangle?'

'Aye, well you see my wife was thinkin' if she could get a bit built on to the house she might start takin' in bed an' breakfasters. Her mother used to do it at one time an' she tells me some of them leave the sheets that clean if you can put them through a mangle you don't need to wash them before you put them back on the beds again.'

155

At twelve there was a break for lunch so we went to join the queue where we were to pay for our purchases and when that was done we discussed arrangements for getting our goods back to Bruach.

'We'll be best hirin' a lorry,' advised Tearlaich. 'I know a man with a lorry would do it for us and then we wouldn't need to wait on the railway.' It sounded a good idea so after arranging to meet us later for a meal Tearlaich and Angy went off to see the man with the lorry while Behag and I indulged in a modest, and, because it proved to be early closing day, a hurried shopping spree. Behag bought a purse for her small daughter, a milk sieve for Morag and a box of cartridges for Hector as well as a frilly blouse for herself and a variety of cakes and 'teabread'. I bought fruit and vegetables and, after a certain amount of hesitation, succumbed at last to permitting myself the luxury of a new alarm clock. We managed to snatch a quick cup of tea before the small café we chose slammed its doors and with an hour to go before we were to meet the two men we sought refuge from the unceasing rain in a nearby church.

'Oh, it's lovely to be off my feet for a while,' sighed Behag. 'I feel as if I'm wearin' sandstone shoes.'

'Slip them off,' I encouraged.

'Will I?' She looked doubtful. 'What will the minister say if he comes in an' sees me?'

'Town ministers are used to it,' I assured her, 'and anyway you'll hear anyone coming.'

She slipped off her shoes and leaned back in the pew, her eyes closed and a contented smile touching her mouth. I wandered round renewing contact with carved wood and chiselled stone, refreshing my memory of skilled craftsmanship, and contrasting it with the utilitarian artefacts of Bruach with their total lack of ornamentation.

'These kind of churches must cost a terrible lot of money,' Behag said when I too went to sit down.

'Yes, but they're beautiful, aren't they?' I replied.

'Morag doesn't like them,' she told me. 'She says she doesn't get the same feelin' of religion in them as in our own.'

We collected 'Joanna' and drove to the restaurant. 'Now this is the way of it,' Tearlaich explained as we were having our pre-departure meal. 'This fellow says he'll collect the stuff first thing in the mornin' as soon as the sale room's open an' he'll take it across the ferry in his own lorry an' have it at Bruach by tomorrow evenin'.'

'It doesn't sound possible,' I said.

'Aye, it's possible right enough. So long as there's no hitch on the way,' replied Tearlaich.

'There's sure to be a hitch,' Angy put in. 'The road to Bruach's as full of hitches as a herrin' net's full of holes.'

'That's because we have to rely on botchers, half the time,' retorted Tearlaich. 'No, you can take it from me there'll be no hitches this time. This fellow's a professional.'

'Is he going to charge a lot for it?'

Tearlaich told us how much and after dividing the cost among us we agreed that though it seemed a lot we must accept that such speedy delivery naturally cost more than goods coming by train, ferry and carrier. We expressed ourselves content with our bargain.

'Here's to Bruach, with beds, mangles, pianos and rugs,' proclaimed Tearlaich gustily as we set off in 'Joanna'. 'An' I believe the rain's lifting at last.'

'An' not before it's time,' said Angy.

'I've been wet inside an' outside for the past twenty-four hours,' confided Tearlaich, producing a half-bottle of whisky. 'I'm no' wantin' to dry out yet.' He put the bottle to his mouth. 'Are you sure you won't take a wee drop yourself?' he asked Behag and me for the second time. We both shook our heads.

'An' did everybody enjoy the roup, then?' he enquired.

'I enjoyed it fine,' replied Behag. 'It was as good as a ceilidh.'

'I enjoyed it too,' I told him. 'The people around me kept me pretty well entertained and the auctioneer was quite amusing too.'

'That auctioneer!' burst out Angy. 'I couldn't get over him. God! the way he could keep on speakin' without takin' a breath an' sayin' the same thing over and over again like a bloody corncake. You'd think he'd wear a hole in his tongue.'

'I can tell you why he can do that,' Tearlaich volunteered.

'Did you know him then?' queried Angy.

'I didn't know him but my uncle worked for this auctioneer's father at one time and I mind my uncle saying how the old man used to breed parrots. He said he used to feed the young birds on a porridge made of maize and oatmeal and they turned out such good talkers he started feeding his children on the same stuff. There's not a one of them that's stopped talking since.'

'Is that true?' asked Behag.

'True as I'm here,' affirmed Tearlaich. 'I know because a fellow was with me during the war and he'd married one of the auctioneer's sisters. He said if he hadn't been called up he would have volunteered because he needed to get away from home for some peace and quiet.'

We took our time on the journey home, calling in to take a strupach once again with Tearlaich's friendly cook and by the time we reached the ferry the rain had ceased and a full moon spread light over the dark water. I flashed 'Joanna's' headlights to indicate we wished to cross.

'It's slow enough comin',' complained Angy after we had waited nearly half an hour. He got out of the car and wandered down the pier. A moment or two later he was back and talking to us through the window. 'I'm seein' a great pile of stuff here waitin' to go across on the ferry,' he informed us in a puzzled voice. 'They're part covered with a tarpaulin but they're pretty wet all the same.'

'It's queer they should be here this time of night,' said Tearlaich. 'What sort of things are they?'

'There's a mattress,' began Angy with commendably restrained glee. 'An' some chairs with a rug on them an' somethin' else pretty big.'

'And that could be a piano?' I questioned with mounting dismay.

'It could well be,' admitted Angy.

'Oh God! I'd best go and see what went wrong,' muttered Tearlaich, struggling out of the car and hurrying down the pier. Behag and I followed.

'That's the way of it,' he confirmed when he and Angy had made a more thorough inspection. 'There's a big crate and one or two other things that's not ours but the rest is what we bought ourselves.' He scratched his head. 'That man swore to me...'

I cut him short. 'Does that mean it will have to stay there out in the open all night?' I demanded.

'Not if I can help it,' responded Tearlaich. The ferry was now nosing into the pier. 'I'll go and see what they have to say.' He threw the words over his shoulder as he went to meet it. Behag and I went back to the car and waited while Tearlaich, Angy and the two ferrymen lifted the tarpaulin. There seemed to be explanations interspersed with protests, arguments and gestures but eventually the tarpaulin was thrown off and the four men, helped now by two youths who had suddenly appeared out of the darkness, carried the goods down the pier and loaded them on the ferry. At last I was able to drive 'Joanna' aboard.

'There was a message from the lorry man,' Tearlaich disclosed. 'Seemingly just after we'd booked him for our lot he had another customer wanting something delivered here urgent tonight so he rushed off to the sale room, loaded up our stuff and brought the whole lot together to save himself another journey. He couldn't get across the ferry because the tide was out so he had to leave it here.'

'I knew there'd be a hitch,' exulted Angy. 'All the same,' he added, 'it's funny he got past without us seein' him.'

'Unless it was while we was takin' our tea,' suggested Behag and we decided that is when it must have been.

'What's going to happen to the stuff when we get it across?' I asked.

'It can stay in the waiting room,' Tearlaich replied. 'It's all right, I've arranged all that.'

It was much too nice a night to waste it on anger or recrimination even if there had been anyone to be angry with. The surrounding hill peaks were washed with moonlight and tiny drifts of tinselled cloud sailed across the sky. It was so calm that one could see the wash of the ferry like a white arc across the water. Behag and I got out of the car.

'I'll tell you what we should do,' said Tearlaich. 'We should get Miss Peckwitt to give us a tune on her piano.'

'Not here,' I demurred but I knew, and I suspected Tearlaich guessed, how quickly I should comply. I was longing to finger those piano keys.

'Come on!' he urged and calling to Angy bade him drag up the long wooden crate which had come along with our own goods to provide me with a seat.

I played first 'Mairi's Wedding' and Tearlaich and Angy started to sing with gusty enthusiasm. When I changed to a reel they pulled Behag into a 'Dashing White Sergeant' and the two youths set each other before leaping into their versions of a Highland Fling. It was a wonderful experience, playing the piano on the open water while the dancers swirled in the moonlight and I enjoyed it so much that I did not know the ferry had cocked a snoot at the island pier and had made three wide circles so as not to berth until the dancers paused for breath. I stopped playing and got back into 'Joanna' ready to drive her ashore.

'I could have listened all night,' approved one of the ferrymen as I passed him. 'I fairly enjoyed that.' Parking 'Joanna' I went to stand beside Behag and watch the unloading of the goods. There came the sound of an engine approaching and a dusty van drove halfway down the pier. Three men alighted from it.

'Is it the corpse you're wantin'?' one of the ferrymen called to them.

'Aye, that's what we're here for,' they confirmed.

'What a time to come for a corpse,' I murmured to Behag. 'I suppose that means the ferry will have to go over and collect it for them?'

'I suppose so,' she assented.

Tearlaich came to stand beside us and I repeated my question to him. He looked distinctly uncomfortable. 'Well, y'see, Miss Peckwitt, it's like this.' He rubbed a self-conscious hand over his chin and with horrid suspicion I followed his glance to where the long wooden crate waited on the otherwise empty ferry.

'Tearlaich!' I almost choked. 'You surely didn't...?'

'I reckon I'd best go and give them a hand,' he said and hurried to join Angy and the three men from the van. I watched, horrified, as they lifted my erstwhile piano stool, carried it off the ferry, past us and up the pier where, not urgently, they loaded it into the waiting van. 'Oh God!' I whimpered and turned to Behag, intent on denouncing both Tearlaich and Angy but seeing her anxious expression I went silently back to the car. She slipped in beside me and I believe had I been able to decide at that moment whether I was more angry than shocked I should have driven off and left the two men to find their own way back to Bruach. As it was I waited until they were in their seats.

161

'Did you know that was a coffin you got me to sit on?' I taxed them.

'Surely we did,' admitted Tearlaich. 'But it wouldn't have given way. It was in a good strong box.'

'You shouldn't have let her do it,' Behag rebuked them. 'Women doesn't take to corpses the same as men. You've upset her.'

'She's easy upset then,' Tearlaich returned impenitently, but he subsided temporarily and we drove for perhaps two miles before he spoke again. 'I'll have a bit of money to give back to you for the lorry,' he said in an attempt at appeasement. 'Seein' we shared the load with a corpse it's goin' to work out a good bit cheaper for us.'

'Oh, shut up about corpses!' I snapped at him.

I heard the sound of a cork being pulled from a bottle. 'I thought you'd be pleased to hear it,' he defended himself.

The carrier delivered my piano and chairs in the late afternoon of the following day, the unprecedentedly quick delivery, so the carrier informed me, being due to the complaints of prospective passengers that they could not get into the ferry waiting room.

'I'll have to go and ask for some help to unload it,' I observed.

'Ach, there's plenty on the way,' he replied. 'They're expectin' you to have a good ceilidh tonight so they'll get finished before they come down.'

'What about you?' I asked.

'Me? I'm waitin' on the ceilidh too.' He took a quick strupach before going to 'look up the lads,' leaving the piano on the lorry parked in front of the cottage. It was about nine and quite dark before anyone arrived to unload and when I went outside with a lantern it seemed to me as if every able-bodied man, woman and child in the village had come to help, impede, encourage or advise. However, the piano defied all attempts to manoeuvre it into my cottage.

'You'll need to higher this door or move one of the stairs,' Erchy reported.

'Then it will just have to go into the barn,' I said sadly, thinking how cold I and my piano were going to be together.

My decision was greeted by something like a cheer. 'All the better,' they assured me. 'We can have a better ceilidh in there than in the cottage.'

'I'm afraid the mice will be making their own ceilidh house in it,' I told them.

'An' there's plenty of room for them too inside it, I'm thinkin',' replied Erchy insensitively.

Once it was in position in the barn about six pairs of hands were punching at the keys and an equal number of feet trying to thump the pedals.

'Give us a tune,' they demanded and to save my piano from complete destruction I agreed immediately. Erchy brought a chair over from the house. 'Seein' you'll be here for the rest of the night you may as well be comfortable,' he told me. I realised the ceilidh had begun. The madman brought along his melodeon; the postman brought his mouth-organ. The young people danced and the elderly watched and gossiped. The barn grew warm and the piano seemed to respond to the exuberance of the dancers, for after an hour's playing I detected no dumb notes and the keys were yielding to the touch of my fingers.

'It's a lovely noise your piano's makin',' someone complimented me enthusiastically at one juncture and when I left the barn to go and supervise the making of tea Hector came in to tell me he thought he'd as soon listen to the piano as to the bagpipes which was praise indeed. By half past four many of the older folk had left save for a few who were still bunched together savouring their tea and gossiping; the young were still cavorting around the barn. I finished playing and slewed round in my chair. Behag was coming towards me with yet another cup of tea. She looked at me quizzically. 'You're tired,' she accused as if she had detected a secret.

The Bruachites considered it discourteous to admit to feeling tired whilst they were in company and managed to give the impression of being fresh and alert until they quite literally keeled over with exhaustion. I was well aware of my own infringement of protocol when I agreed ruefully that I was very tired indeed. It had been a long and heavy day following directly upon the excitement of the journey and I was aching for my bed.

Behag turned to Janet. 'I'm thinkin' it's time we was away to our beds. Miss Peckwitt says she's tired.'

'Oh yes, indeed,' agreed Janet with instant sympathy. She raised her voice. 'Come away home now, everybody. We're keepin' Miss Peckwitt from her bed.'

The dancers turned to me with looks of consternation. 'She cannot be tired,' Tearlaich denied. 'She's done nothing but sit and play all evening.'

'I am,' I insisted.

'Go to your bed then!' commanded Erchy with a cheeky glint in his eye. 'We'll carry on by ourselves. We still have the melodeon.'

'Here, no indeed,' said Janet, shocked by his rudeness.

'One more dance, then!' shouted the postman, tucking his mouth-organ into his pocket and pulling me into the centre of the dance floor.

'Last dance!' called Erchy authoritatively. 'Eightsome reel, an' keep it goin' till you drop!' he instructed the roadman. The melodeon played on until at last the roadman sat back, his arms dropping at his sides, his head shaking a tired refusal to commands to 'carry on'.

There was a procession to the cottage to retrieve coats and gumboots and then everyone returned to join hands for 'Auld Lang Syne'. I never knew until then that 'Auld

Lang Syne' had so many verses but at last it was over and, unhooking the lantern from the rafter, I followed my friends outside.

'Good night!' I called again and again in response to their receding farewells and, thankful to see the very last guest depart, I secured the gate against trespassing cattle. My mind was already so obsessed with the desire for sleep that there was difficulty in convincing myself of the chores I must attend to before I could give in. I banked up the fire; filled the kettle; wound the alarm clock; put out the kitchen lamp. It was only eight steps now to my bedroom where I could drop my clothes, turn out the lamp and tumble into the blessed sanctuary of my bed.

As I opened the bedroom door I discovered that the last of my guests had not gone. Indeed the last of my guests was wrapped in my eiderdown fast asleep on my bed. I was so cross at being thwarted that the tears came into my eyes.

'Get out of my bed!' I snapped.

The muffled voice of Tearlaich came from the bundle. 'Ach, I was tired.'

'I'm tired too,' I replied, 'and I want to go to bed.'

'So do I, my darlin'.' The response was cheerful. 'I've been wantin' to all evening. Come and cuddle beside me.'

He lifted the eiderdown invitingly and revealed lying beside him a bottle of whisky pushed into one of his boots. The other boot was still on his foot. I had heard of champagne being drunk out of a lady's slipper but whisky out of a boot seemed too preposterous even for Tearlaich. He started muttering in Gaelic and though I could not decide what he was saying his tone sounded distinctly seductive. I gave him a push.

'Everyone else is away home to their beds and you must go too,' I shouted into his ear. 'Your mother will wonder what on earth's happened to you.' It wasn't true, of course.

Hospitality in Bruach was such that mothers did not have to wonder where their sons spent the night.

'I'm hellish drunk,' admitted Tearlaich, rolling over.

'I know you are and you'll be downright ashamed of yourself tomorrow. You won't dare to look me in the face for a week.' That would certainly be true. I put down the alarm clock and went downstairs to make him a cup of black coffee and while I was about it I opened the door to listen for signs that some of his friends might still be within hailing distance. There was only a soft sweep of wind and a scattering of stars throwing a faint shimmer over the sea. I cupped my hands to my mouth and yelled as loudly as I could hoping that somewhere some of my erstwhile guests would hear me and come to my aid. No response broke the silence of the night.

I took the coffee upstairs and persuaded Tearlaich to sit up. Shaking his head and squinting through his tousled hair like a bemused calf he took up the cup and after drinking about half of it started to ramble jerkily about love and how good it would be for me but as his eyes were screwed tight shut the whole time it was plain he had no idea whom he was addressing. The cup was tilting dangerously and to save my eiderdown I took it from him whereupon he grabbed the whisky bottle, drained it and settled down to sleep again.

I gave up, resolving to leave him there and make up the bed in the spare room for myself but as I was taking the blankets from the chest I heard voices outside and the kitchen door was flung open. Someone was bumping about in the dark. I was halfway down the stairs when Erchy's voice called: 'Have you seen that bugger Tearlaich? We've lost him.'

'He's upstairs in my bed,' I called testily. 'And I hope you'll be able to drag him out of it. He's a damn nuisance.'

I lit the way upstairs and Erchy, assisted by the roadman, pulled the protesting Tearlaich off the bed and put on his boot. Leaving me with the empty whisky bottle as a memento they hauled him down the stairs and outside.

'That's no' a nice thing to do at all, man,' Erchy chided as they struggled to get him through the gate.

The reproof sobered Tearlaich momentarily. 'What wasn't?' he asked stupidly.

'To take a woman's bed an' not let her into it,' retorted Erchy.

'I would have let her into it,' objected Tearlaich defensively. 'I'd have made it cosy for her.'

'Ach, if folks behave like that Miss Peckwitt will be packing her bags an' goin' back to where she came from,' Erchy told him.

Tearlaich's dragging feet dug into the ground, halting his supporters. He struggled round to face me.

'You'll not go back to that backwards place, Miss Peckwitt?' he pleaded apologetically.

'To what backwards place?' I asked, smiling despite myself.

'England,' replied Tearlaich.

I laughed outright then. 'Oh, no,' I assured him. 'I'm not thinking of doing that for a long time.'

'I wouldn't...' began Tearlaich but Erchy cut in with 'Ach, come on, man! I'm wantin' my bed.' He and the roadman shouldered Tearlaich between them and as their footsteps merged into a rhythm Tearlaich broke into a song. I went back indoors, intent again on the prospect of bed and the few hours' sleep I hoped would chase some of the weariness from my limbs. As my hand was on the bedroom door my new alarm clock, set for half past seven, made me jump with its raucous ringing.

It was time to start another day.

LILLIAN BECKWITH

THE BAY OF STRANGERS

In these eight short stories Lillian Beckwith packs in a rich cast of characters and seductive Highland settings. In the title story Catriona McRae embarks on married life and learns a closely guarded secret from her mother-in-law. 'The Banjimolly' features a witch – and two bottles of whisky. 'Because of an Elephant' concerns an eccentric laird's wife. A boy and his adored collie dog, Meg, are the subjects of 'The Last Shot'. Each story is beautifully and affectionately told.

BEAUTIFUL JUST!

On the Hebridean island of Bruach, life among the crofters is as happy and full of humour as ever. Beckwith tells enchanting tales about the islanders' wit, their canny resourcefulness and their gossipy interest in outsiders. There is Flora and the fancy-dress dance, beachcombing, winkle-gathering, Highland cattle and a stag – among many other characters and animals. Based on Beckwith's own experiences.

'hilarious' – *The Sunday Times*

'absorbing…its humour is happy, easy and natural'
– *The Mirror*

LILLIAN BECKWITH

BRUACH BLEND

Meet some familiar – and some less familiar – inhabitants of Bruach. Back with more comical escapades are Erchy and Morag, the philandering Hector and Hamish, with his unusual talent for nursing lambs. We meet also Bonny the cow, Crumley the bull, and Harry the hedgehog, which make up 'Miss Peckwitt's colourful and uncontrollable collection of animals and other livestock'.

'A book which leaves you with a warm, happy glow. Her Highland crofters emerge from the pages as true friends'
– *The Mirror*

'How can anyone read this book without being convulsed with laughter and admiration?' – *Eastern Daily Press*

THE HILLS IS LONELY

When Lillian Beckwith advertised for a secluded place in the country, she received a letter with the following unusual description of an isolated Hebridean croft: 'Surely it's that quiet even the sheeps themselves on the hills is lonely and as to the sea it's that near as I use it myself everyday for the refusals...'

Her curiosity aroused, Beckwith took up the invitation. This is the comic and enchanting story of the strange rest cure that followed and her efforts to adapt to a completely different way of life.

'A bouquet for Miss Beckwith' – Eric Linklater

LILLIAN BECKWITH

THE LOUD HALO

In *The Loud Halo* Lillian Beckwith serves up another delightful slice of Hebridean life and a collection of local characters. Meet Johnny Comic, Morag, Kirsty, Behag, Hector, Erchy and the postie – among others. Subjects for amusement include tourists, an election, blizzards and a tinker's wedding. Each episode is told with wit and affection.

'A sparkling book which could well become a Scottish humorous classic' – *Weekly Scotsman*

THE SEA FOR BREAKFAST

Lillian Beckwith's settling in on the island of Bruach and having a croft of her own, is the basis of these comic adventures. Adapting to a totally different way of life provides many excuses for humour and the eccentric cast of characters guarantees there is never a dull moment on Bruach. In one story beachcombing yields a strange find. In another a Christmas party results in a riotous night's celebrations.

'The most amusing book to come my way' – *The Sunday Times*

'It would be very difficult not to enjoy *The Sea for Breakfast*...for the charm and simplicity of its writing, not to mention the wonderful, warm people who inhabit its covers' – *The Scotsman*